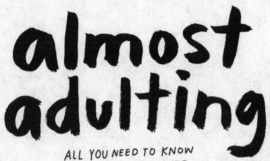

almost adulting

ALL YOU NEED TO KNOW TO GET IT TOGETHER (SORT OF)

almost adulting

ALL YOU NEED TO KNOW
TO GET IT TOGETHER
(SORT OF)

ARDEN ROSE

HARPER
An Imprint of HarperCollinsPublishers

Library of Congress Control Number: 2017930902

www.epicreads.com

ISBN 978-0-06-257411-4

Typography by David Curtis

Illustration by Carolyn Suzuki & Hannah Jacobs

21 22 PC/LSCH 10 9 8 7 6 5 4

❖

First paperback edition, 2018

This book is for those of us who still burn the popcorn,

don't know when the electric bill is due,

and who never quite learned how to calculate the tip in their

heads. Cheers to the almost adults.

Table of Contents

Well hey, guys. The past year has been INSANE. The support you've all shown for this precious book of mine has been overwhelming and special. While writing *Almost Adulting*, I kept imagining my younger self reading it. I tried to tap into what exactly I missed out on when I was eighteen. What were the life lessons that went over my head? Or the ones I blatantly ignored because I was a cocky little shit who thought she knew everything already? Every topic I cover in *Almost Adulting*—from my very own sex talk, to a candid chat about my dad being an awesome dude—ended up being cathartic and soothing in some way. It was like I had all these free-form memories that I'd never pulled out of the depths of my head. Every time I tried to put myself in my (admittedly angsty) teen self's shoes, I came out with memories that otherwise would have been buried forever. Writing gave me a chance to scoop up buckets of past thoughts and feelings and pour them onto pages. The book ended up being a confessional, a diary, and a form of therapy that I'm incredibly appreciative of.

As for the reception for *Almost Adulting*, it's mind-boggling. Every time I check the notifications on my various social media accounts, I'm surprised to see more and more posts mentioning the book! The creativity that has gone into each of these posts is downright heart-warming. The fact that you not only want to read my book but also show it off to your friends and followers is kind and sweet. All the curled-up cats and dogs I've seen nestled up against my book make me want to smile endlessly. I swear you guys have the best taste in pets, Instagram filters, and books. I'm incredibly grateful for each and every picture, tweet, Instagram, or blog that has included *Almost Adulting*. The social support you showed made my book what it is today. Thank you for exceeding my expectations with my first (but hopefully not last) book.

Love,
Arden

LET'S GET IT STARTED IN HERE

When I was nine, adult looked like my parents. At fourteen, adult looked like my brother studying for college exams. At age eighteen, adult looked like women who could get into bars without fake IDs. As a twenty-one-year-old, adult has come to mean something new and strange. Because, as it turns out, I've been adulting for quite some time without even realizing it.

I always thought that once you reach a particular age or some particular milestone in life, a stranger runs up to you, slams a stack of papers into your chest, and exclaims, "You've been served!" Upon closer examination, these very official documents detail the intricacies of applying for adulthood. After several days of intense administration, sleepless nights trying to remember your social security number, and bouts of carpal tunnel, you've completed your application. You wait anxiously in line at the post office with all the other prospective adults and then cast your entry into the abyss of the postal service system, hoping a reassuring letter will be delivered promptly to you in response.

You immediately start thinking of all the things you could do with your very own adulthood. What kind of path-altering confidence will you gain? It could change the very fabric of your life! One day you will order a margarita without hastily adding the word "virgin." You might be able to have a conversation with your overly religious mother without profusely sweating five minutes in. You consider all the impressive retorts you'll be able to spew at your nosy friends when they won't leave you alone about your obsession with cats on Instagram. You might even be able to make a compelling argument about the benefits of following Grumpy Cat WITHOUT STUTTERING.

I know. Right now you get the creeping suspicion that your life kinda blows, being a youth and all. Being young and hungry and unsure isn't as fun as promised. The word "teenager" doesn't have the same intrigue it had at thirteen. You envy your older friends who have their lives perfectly in order, like a well-managed Bed Bath & Beyond. You wonder when your organizational skills and willpower will kick in. It seems as though everyone who could be seen as adult has their life moving along at the pace of a properly programmed machine. "Maybe that's what it means to be an adult," you ponder. "Having your shit together. Yeah, that must be it!" You see older people with jobs and cars and houses and families, and you think of the stability and poise that must follow.

All you want is entry into a club that everyone older seems to have been surreptitiously welcomed into. You start to wonder why you haven't been ushered into it, too. After all, your application for adulthood was put forward weeks ago! You worry you might not have what it takes. You think back on your recent actions. So, yes, last month, you did turn your used underwear inside out instead of doing laundry. And then you wore that used inside-out underwear. For three days. CRAP. How could someone with such a clear lack of self-respect and hygiene be considered an elite adult? When you look around at the crisp shirts, company credit cards, and family vacations, it all looks vaguely foreign and intimidating. You never should have sent in your application in the first place!!!

Adulthood must be a much tougher road than you made it out to be in your addled little pea brain. If they're going to make you do dishes and dust things every now and then, what other atrocities must follow? Attending high school acquaintances' lackluster weddings? Downloading and subsequently subjecting your heart to dating apps like Tinder? God forbid you have to make a doctor's appointment over the phone. You might have to call Dr. Wheeler for a dentist appointment BY YOURSELF???

No.

You begin to regret your initial greediness. Is there anyone you can call to get your application canceled? You are not ready for adulthood, and adulthood is not ready for you. You begin asking around, trying to figure out at what age people usually get accepted into adulthood. Everyone seems to have a different number. Some say twenty-one. Others say thirty. You hope it's thirty. Yeah, you have a good feeling about thirty. You obsessively calculate the time you have left, running your own childlike wonder of the world down like an hourglass, the last grains of sand slipping to the bottom. You start noticing everyone's age. The number of child prodigies coming out of the woodwork on the news is worrying you. Your mom sends you a video on Facebook. It's an interview with an eleven-year-old from Tennessee about her re-creation of the Sistine Chapel in her family's small southern home. It's beautiful. It brings you to tears. Not because of the majesty of the painting itself, but because of the lack of success you've had in comparison. She painted it when she was ten. She says she's gotten better since then. You've gotten better at not picking your nose since you were ten. Each brushstroke she issues while making her latest masterpiece (probably the fucking *Mona Lisa*) swipes away a fragment of your young potential. You're left feeling inadequate. Outdated. Used.

The next day, a small envelope arrives on your

doorstep. Your name is coldly printed in plain block letters on the front. Your shaky hands pick up and hold the letter in disbelief, denial, and dread. *Is this it? Has my fate been sealed by the Big Brother–like authorities enforcing adulthood?* As you tentatively pry apart the adhesive-edged envelope, you question how you got to this place. What could have possessed you to willingly apply to the never-ending process of aging? You were once so bright, so alive. An abundance of wasted potential. You probably could have been in the Olympics for gymnastics or diving. Probably. You slowly pull the edge of a folded piece of paper from the ominous sheath. Your heart races as your blurry vision tries to make sense of the shapes forming words on the page.

OVERDUE BILL NOTICE. If you do not submit payment for your previous parking violation, we hereby notify you that your license will be sus–

You crumple up the page and toss it into the pile of other papers you've been willfully avoiding. You promise yourself that tomorrow will be your admin day, in which you'll snap into an organizational robot. How forward-thinking of you! You silently give yourself a pat on the back even though you hadn't done anything yet.

You make your way into the kitchen, searching the pantry for an appropriate meal to help you forget about the parking ticket. You spy a half-stale box of Double Stuf Oreos. You consider grabbing a plate to partition a reasonable portion of cookies, then scoff at the thought. As if you have any semblance of self-control. You take your dinner and swaddle yourself in blankets on the living room couch. Gorging on your meal of choice, you flick through the latest array of movies on Netflix. Your nightly ritual commences: Eat. Watch. Sleep.

You're not a sad case. You're just a human being with a basic need to relax after a long day. You look around and notice that your plants are getting a bit wilt-y. But you know you can wait a good two more days before things get to the point of no return. You've killed more plants than you can count and have finally resigned yourself to a succulents-only lifestyle. One day a mysterious white fuzz is going to creep up on your cactus. You will, as you always do, watch in detachment as the poor thing is devoured over a month of agony. You will buy a new cactus the next day in a bright-blue pot.

And that, right there, is the moment. Without being conscious of it, you are an adult. You've been adulting all along. You might not feel any different than when you were thirteen and footloose and fancy free, but you are. You have responsibilities now—even if you actively ignore them constantly. You are relied upon to be a real human and do real human things, and if that isn't the definition of adulting, my life is a lie.

In the pages that follow, I'm going to attempt to validate you. We're going to discuss sex, romance, feng shui-ing your living space, and all things in between. By the end, I want you to feel like the wonderful, capable goddess you are. Being an adult isn't as scary and intimidating as it seems. You've probably been a full-blown grown-up for a while without realizing it. Now we can just finesse your individuality and figure out what makes you the interesting son of a bitch that everyone wants to get to know. So let's do this thing, reader. Let's figure out what almost adulting means to you.

Let's not forget that everything you read in this book is from my perspective. Your opinion about sex or interior decorating might be different from mine. That's totally fine and dandy, and I actively encourage you to question my own thoughts and feelings toward life. So sit back, grab a large mug of tea, and let's get into it!

THE THINGS YOU ABSOLUTELY MOST DEFINITELY NEED TO KNOW ABOUT BEING AN ADULT

Adulting can be an arduous journey to undertake, and there are several things you're going to need in order to navigate these murky waters. Obviously you need to go buy toilet paper and always have trash bags (Amazon Prime is going to be your new best friend), but there's so much more to being adequately prepared for adulthood. First and foremost, learn how to use a washing machine. I have no patience for people unable to use either a dishwasher or a washing machine. THE BUTTONS ARE SO SELF-EXPLANATORY. Also, have you ever just, I don't know, problem-solved for once and done something for yourself? I've been doing my own laundry since I was twelve. Granted I had a medium-sized family that required an "every man for himself" mentality, but c'mon. I'd say the majority of offenders in this particular domestic realm are guys, but I've seen some girls really screw the pooch when it comes to separating lace and things with aggressive zippers. Honey, it's called a lingerie bag. Get one! Your non-holey underwear will thank you!

I don't mean to be hypercritical. This is supposed to be a safe space for those who want to learn in a nonjudgmental environment. But get your damn domestic god and goddess on, people. Embrace cleaning and chores because they are your new reality! Don't make it something that drags you down, just get it done. Do the stuff you hate first. I HATE doing the dishes. Hate it. Hell is an endless stream of soggy food remnants, crusty yet oozy at the same time, sticking to dish after dish while I inhale the smell of sour milk in forgotten cereal bowls and day-old chili. Oily separation swirls above a sea of emulsified beans as I scrape and wash and pray to all the gods that there won't be another dish after this one. But nay, it continues, the never-ending deluge of filth that I have

wrought on myself. God, I hate dishes. But they must be done, so I've learned to breathe through my mouth, put on some Beyoncé, and get on with the damn thing.

That's one lesson real life teaches you. Most of the people who seem like they have their lives in order are also the people who are great at doing things they don't want to do. That's why teachers giving you busywork isn't such a terrible thing. Let me explain before I alienate a large group of you all at once. So much of schoolwork is doing something you don't want to do, on a deadline you don't want to make. But you do it anyway. You do the homework, you make the grade, and then it happens again and again until you have a degree in second-century Roman history and a mountain of student debt. But hey! You learned something! And not just how to tie a toga (not sure what else you would learn in second-century Roman history), but something so much more important than that: how to do things that aren't fun.

Our modern world tells us that "having fun" is what makes us happy. That traveling, seeing the world, eating the best food, and having sex with the hottest bodies is going to make us content. This is simply not true. I know many privileged people who travel the world constantly, "having fun" in various amazing locations that we simple folk could only DREAM of. But more often than not, these people are never joyful. Having what you want all the time is a hidden curse. You end up spending your days chasing the best things, only to have the most breath-taking experiences feel . . . meh. There's no balance to make the pleasure enjoyable. You didn't work for it. The release and joy that come from luxury are only felt when you earned it. Ask any spoiled rich kid riding on a golden hoverboard about his trip to Bora-Bora last summer and you'll probably hear the same thing every time: "It was all right. The masseuse wasn't as great as the one in Saint-Tropez. And there weren't as many topless ladies."

That kid never worked for that vacation or those naked women. Someone else worked their ass off to provide him with the luxurious life he leads. In short, we all want to be the spoiled rich kid, but working and doing the tedious admin of life is rewarding, even if it feels soul crushing at the time. So just know that every time you do the dishes, or pay your bills on time, or talk to your overly concerned mother for more than twenty minutes, you're paying it forward to a much bigger prize. When you're lying on a budget beach in Cancún with an empty beer can an inch away from your head and a lightly used tampon just a couple feet farther, you'll feel ten times better than whatever turd social climber is getting rubbed down in the Bahamas. You know why? Because you EARNED that crappy beach. You worked toward that vacation. And you should be proud that you made it there all by yourself! No help from Mom and Dad. That beach weekend is all on you. You deserve to be chugging four-dollar margaritas in the sun for twelve hours, so do it. Just don't forget to wear sunscreen. And drink plenty of water.

Speaking of drinking plenty of water, let's move on to the next essential of adulthood: taking care of yourself, mind and body. This is something that took an enormous amount of time for me to understand. I used to dissociate food and health on an unhealthy level. Every time I went grocery shopping, I would throw all the leafy greens and papayas and chia seeds into my cart, only to have them rot on a shelf in my kitchen as I ate Oreos. Goddamn

Oreos. They will be the death of me. I've since come to understand that I only have one body and one mind in this life, and I need to take care of both of them. Even though Oreos are vegan (I don't even want to know how that's possible), they will not fulfill your daily nutritional requirements. It's time to understand that you determine how your body and mind operate at any given time based on what you're fueling it with. I know that might sound crazy, but if you're eating triple-decker burgers with an avalanche of aioli oozing out the sides every day, you're going to die a deliciously young death. Sorry! It's true! There's no better time than right now to start taking care of yourself and understanding how food can affect your entire being.

That being said, I'm still on my own journey toward being completely happy with my routine, so I'm not going to stand on my soapbox and make you feel like a terrible person for eating ninety grapefruits a day or whatever. (I can't entirely remember what diet we're supposed to be mad about right now.) What I can tell you is to do your research. Educate yourself on your diet and see if what you're eating is the best option for your body. We're in a day and age where mountains of research are at our disposal. Soak it in! Even if some of it can be hard truths (like Oreos being both vegan and probably created through a satanic ritual), the fact that you're ingesting knowledge surrounding your daily intake is so important.

I don't mean that you need to read every book obsessing over a plant-based diet, but it is a good idea to allow yourself to entertain ideas. Being completely closed off to a philosophy or lifestyle is not a very adult-y thing to do. In fact, it's an incredibly childish way to look at the world. You might say, "My grandfather has eaten the same meat-and-potato breakfast for the past thirty years and he's as fit as a fiddle!" Well, your grandfather is also intensely homophobic and doesn't understand why segregated bathrooms aren't still a thing. Being open-minded to ideas different from your current ideas is never a bad thing. You can entertain something without adhering to it. That is how we grow and learn. Remember when you were little and you wouldn't eat Brussels sprouts because your mom boiled them? Roast those bad boys with chili flakes, salt, and pepper. Add a spritz of lemon once they're out of the oven and BAM! Why did you ever hate them in the first place? Because you weren't open to trying a new strategy.

Essential number three, and arguably the most important thing you need to take into adulthood, is openness.
Being able to entertain new ideas, thoughts, or activities
without immediately recoiling in terror is incredibly
important to having a happy adulthood. This is a princi-
ple you can take with you throughout life, and it makes
things so much more enjoyable. Being an easygoing person isn't about not caring what happens to you. It's about
being able to let go of past assumptions and allow new
experiences even if they're foreign or scary. You need to
start trusting yourself more. Trust in the fact that your

judgment is good enough to allow different life paths without them being scary. Go on that five-mile hike with an overly athletic friend. Yeah, you might get your ass kicked by nature, but at least you're willing to try. And, who knows! You might end up loving a good romp through the wilderness. But when in doubt: do it for the Instagram.

Your twenties aren't that scary after all. My boobs aren't yet sagging, and I'm not pulling gray hairs out, and I can see my late twenties operating a lot like my current life. I've been living on my own, making microwave mac 'n' cheese like a boss. I've filed several tax returns, and I've considered tax evasion every time. I've packed up and transported my entire apartment without a moving service. I've taken at least four different people to the hospital, including myself. I adopted a cat off the streets of Crenshaw. I gave that cat to my brother less than a year later.

The most important things I've learned in the last couple years all came from making mistakes and getting messy. Thanks, Ms. Frizzle, for teaching me that lesson early on in life. I was a disaster so that you, dear reader, don't have to be as much of a disaster as I was.

No one really knows what they're doing, and I find a bizarre comfort in that. After all, you can't judge yourself for being such a fuckup when you know that everyone else is struggling just as hard to be a normal human with responsibilities.

Top Tips for Not Giving a Shit

- Think about the billions of people who currently exist and how little you care if they get a nipple piercing.
- People generally don't have the attention span or ability to think past themselves to judge you constantly for your slipups in life. So learn from your stupid mistakes and let others do the same.
- No one pays enough attention to the important things in life. Put your valuable time and energy into the major issues. Like finding a way to genetically engineer miniature elephants to have as domesticated house pets.
- You're your own best friend in life. Treat yourself with kindness.
- Just do whatever it is that you're second-guessing. Unless the thing you are contemplating doing is meth. Don't do meth.
- Realize that you can't let the feelings of others make you live less.

MY MOM ISN'T GOING TO GROCERY SHOP FOR ME ANYMORE??

Before I moved out on my own, I thought I had it all together. I was young, had more than fifteen dollars in my savings account, and knew everything I needed to know to be a successful young hotshot. At eighteen I thought I was going to be married by twenty-one, a mom by twenty-five (ha-ha-ha), and a millionaire by thirty. The year I graduated from high school, I decided I was going to move to Hollywood to pursue my budding YouTube career.

After living on my own in LA for the past three years, I can now say that eighteen was the stupidest, most educational year of my life. No one told me adulting was less about setting age goals and having your shit together, and more about holding a random girl's hair as she vomits in your bathroom on your boyfriend's twenty-second birthday because she's eighteen and doing exactly what every girl her age is doing: not having her shit together. I can't judge. I've slept wrapped around more toilets than men.

This isn't to say I was always a total mess. I was a gradually worsening mess. I started off pretty good. I was raised by two very intelligent, respectable southern Christians who taught me right from wrong and how to repress my accent when I slipped and said the word *y'all* in mixed company. My parents were supportive, but very good at letting their kids do their own thing. I remember telling them I had created and started uploading videos online at fourteen. They either figured I was too smart to be lured in by an internet predator or that, with four kids, if I ended up in some kidnapper's basement, they had three more chances.

I'm totally kidding. (Sort of.)

My parents just wanted their children to be autonomous beings. If I chose to sit in my room watching

Shakira videos while scratching my ass, they were happy to let me. I'm so grateful for that. I'm so grateful my mom and dad wanted me to do my own thing. Without their relentless trust in and respect for me, I never would have had the blind courage to leave home so early and skip out on college. Although, now that I'm thinking about it, they might have been happy to have a non-kidnapping-related reason for them not to spend fifty grand on my education. . . .

So I'm eighteen and I have a burgeoning internet career that lets me pay for rent and a couple bags of Flamin' Hot Cheetos a month. I packed three comically large suitcases, signed a lease on a small apartment in Hollywood with a girl I'd never met before, and hopped on a plane. I had this weird idea when I was younger that I was some kind of born-to-be nomad, able to pick up and move without constant homesickness or worry. Because I was from a small town in the South, I always dreamed of traveling to huge, magnificent cities and bumming it couch to couch, exploring the world. My younger self had a lower sense of self-preservation and less overall wariness of strangers. I felt as though nothing could touch me once I was out in the real world. For whatever reason, I thought my "street smarts" (as if I had anything remotely anticipatory or observant about me) would make me invincible. I couldn't be duped! I couldn't be swindled! I was the smartest eighteen-year-old who ever lived. I truly believed that I would be happy anywhere I had a place to lay my head at night. Unless that place ended up being bug-infested.

It was only when my water was turned off and I was eating saltines out of a plastic bag, crying on the phone to my mom, that I understood how silly I was to think I could take on this world solo-dolo. Turns out I am not one of the few who can live completely autonomously after being babied for my entire life. (Go figure!) Since I was born, I'd had someone looking out for me and packing me nutritionally balanced school lunches every morning. It wasn't until I was completely on my own with parents a six-hour flight away that I realized how much work goes into adulting. Things don't magically stay clean. Dust accumulates. Bills pile up. You start hiding traffic tickets from yourself so you can feel like they don't exist anymore.

(Quick tip: PAY YOUR TICK-ETS. About four months into my new California lifestyle of glamour and luxury, I got pulled over in my dented 2010 Nissan Versa outside Ventura County. I proceeded to put off paying the three-hundred-dollar ticket because I felt naive for falling for a speed trap. Lame excuse, but I ended up willfully forgetting about the ticket and nearly going to court over my license being suspended. Case in point, PAY THE DAMN TICKET. Don't put it in a cup holder and spill coffee all over it. Don't shove it angrily in your car door's side pocket only to throw it away in a sporadic cleaning spree a month later. Pay. It.)

Obviously ticket payment is a serious issue, but there are several only slightly more important points to remember when moving out and living on your own. First and foremost, ask a crap-ton of questions. As you've (hopefully) figured out by now, no one has their life together completely. This includes you. You don't know everything, and you never will! But there are some people who have ample life experience and a great fondness for you. Generally these people are your parental figures. Not sure if you know this, but they tend to love you and want you to succeed. So ask them about everything. By everything I mean EVERYTHING. I can't tell you how many times I put important tasks on hold just so I could pretend like I could do things on my own and avoid asking understandable questions. Here's what an average conversation with my dad sounded like at the time:

> **Father:** "Have you gotten your oil changed like I've been asking you to for the last three weeks?"
>
> **Me:** "It's just been a hectic few weeks. I promise I'll do it this weekend."
>
> **Father:** "Your car is going to catch on fire if you don't change the oil. Do you need me to explain how to change your oil again?"
>
> **Me:** *sweats nervously trying to find a way to get the information without seeming like a forgetful idiot*
>
> **Father:** "Okay . . . ? Well, you know I love you, and if you need any help, you can call me."
>
> **Me:** *internally screams while trying to swallow my pride and ask what the hell a drain plug is*

Father: *"Mom is worried about you. Call me next week when your oil is changed."*

You may say, "Hey, Arden! Have you heard about this thing called Wikihow? It's this real neat internet site where they teach you how to do literally anything, including milking a cat. Try your luck with that."

To that I say, I KNOW, OKAY. But there's nothing like real-life-person knowledge to help you out. The way people explain things in person is far superior to some faceless internet text. I need humanity! I need my dad!

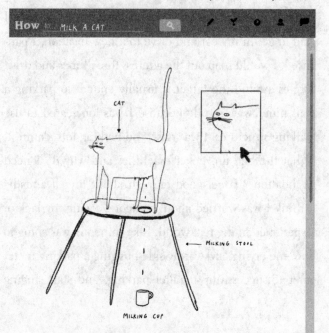

In this case, I didn't actually need good ole Jett Ricks to get my oil changed. I just needed to drive my car to Jiffy Lube or some other purveyor of car oil. The problem was, I was fearful. Which leads me to my next piece of advice: when you move out and start functioning on your own, you need to grow a pair. Ovaries, testes—I'm not a picky lady. Just grow something. You have to suck it up and do the thing that you don't know how to do and are therefore terrified of doing. I might be a wimpy exception to the rule, but I was so terrified to drive anywhere after I moved. Granted, I moved to LA, where parking is the equivalent of a finger up the butt, but every time I had to get in my car and drive to a new location, I panicked. I would map out the address three times and drive circles around the target. I usually ended up parking a half mile away, mostly because I was too scared to use parking structures. I was raised on parking lots, damn it! What the hell are ticket machines and why do I need "validation"? I feel good enough about myself already! I think I was worried about someone seeing my lack of experience in the real world. Like someone was going to spot me crying, awkwardly side-hugging a parking meter after unsuccessfully parallel parking, and start singing

"Another One Bites the Dust" spitefully in my direction. I had this weird feeling that all eyes were on me when I was learning how to assimilate into LA society.

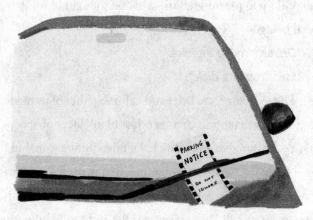

Fortunately, I got used to the parking structure thing after unsuccessfully parking on the wrong floor several times, only to have no parking spaces available when I went to get closer to the entrance. Just to give you some peace of mind, if you're anything like me and freak out at the idea of taking more than five seconds to parallel park, people can get over themselves. I've had to learn the hard way that driving is all about not giving a fuck. The other day, I had the right of way and turned right at a stop sign.

Unbeknownst to me, another car had been waiting a half second longer than me to turn from the opposite side. Lucky me, the road ahead was two lanes going in the same direction next to each other, and the driver decided to pull up to me and tell me what he thought of my general being.

Driver: *"You're an idiot."*

Me: *"You're a dick."*

The exchange was brief and calm. Neither of us made any show of emotion or anger. Just blank faces of acceptance. I'm an idiot. He's a dick. I tend to think I won, but I still spent the next hour contemplating why he would say something so mean. I'm just a girl trying to make it in this big, scary world! What gives you the right to belittle me so absolutely? What did I REALLY do wrong? Where did I mess up in my life so terribly that I am an "idiot"? Am I an idiot? He certainly believes that. He's probably seen a few idiots in his day. Granted, he was holding a Monster Energy in one hand and the steering wheel of a janked-out 2007 Corolla in the other, but he must know better than me! Ultimately, very embarrassingly, I ended up crying into the shoulder of my poor boyfriend. I couldn't help it! All of a sudden I felt shocked and exposed by those three insidious little words.

Since then, I've decided that I am no longer going to let other people get to me, on the road or in life. It's not worth it! I felt so guilty and ashamed and upset by something that was a blip on the radar of that guy's day. I was letting an insignificant insult bore a hole right through my skull, and I was sick of feeling so exposed every time I "messed up" in public. We empathetic, overthinking individuals always get the harsh, mean, short end of the stick. It's not fair, and it's not fun. But like I said before, you gotta grow a pair. Or thick skin. Or thick skin on your pair. And now I'll stop while I'm ahead.

Once you're on your own in a city you're unfamiliar with, it's time to get a little selfish. It might go against everything your God-fearing parents instilled in you, but looking after Numero Uno can become a very necessary reality if you're anything like me. Mom and Dad aren't here to back you up when things get hairy this time. Part of the problem was that my parents taught me to be polite to a fault. When I was younger, I would roll over in any confrontation. If someone needed something from me, I gave it to them. This once resulted in me giving away a three-hundred-dollar purse because a "friend" thought it would look good on her for an event. She never gave back that bag, and I'm still bitter. If I called three years after the fact, do you think she'd still have it? I should shake her down for it, honestly. But that's a Future Arden idea. Past Arden was too much of a pushover to ever put herself first.

Through the years, I've come to the conclusion that everyone is a narcissistic jerk at heart. We all just want what's best for ourselves. Some people express that desire more than others. My constant rolling over was a defense mechanism to make other humans like me. It benefited me if they saw my kindness as genuine and all-encompassing. They'd be more likely to do kind things back if I did them first. Kinda twisted, but being selfless was a form of selfishness in my life. Not that I knew I was being manipulative or anything; I just didn't know any other way to operate. I was so uncertain about how to effectively communicate my thoughts and needs that I ultimately helped people in the hopes that they might notice I needed help, too. This led to too many misreadings of social situations, and a whole lot of me running myself down to try and constantly be in the service of others.

Over time, I've learned it's better to just be honest in any situation. Don't be bullheaded or rage against people constantly, but you don't have to give away every bit of yourself to benefit someone else. That's not going to help you or the other person in the long run. Do what you can to help others, but don't begin to feel like you're constantly babying or caretaking other people. (Unless you actually make your living as a babysitter or hospice worker.) Be reasonable with your own powers and your expectations of others. If you wouldn't expect someone to clean out your kitchen for free on a Saturday night, don't do it for someone else. I once legit spent a weekend being a free cleaner for a friend who wanted to go out and party. Why? Because I wanted to be liked. I would fill her apartment with Jell-O if she asked me to do that today. You're not at anyone's beck and call. You're an autonomous being who deserves respect.

Being an adult is realizing that other people are not better or above you. We're all just humans who make mistakes and don't have the whole picture. People are going to be mean and petty and make you uncomfortable, but you have the power to undercut their influence on you. So, no, you don't have to think you're an idiot just because some dude says you are! He doesn't know you. He sees such a tiny portion of your expansive ongoing life. On the flip side, you don't know him. Maybe he pulled up to a stop sign to turn left and go to the ice-cream shop he and his ex-boyfriend used to go to every day together. He just wanted a taste of the sea salt and pistachio flavor that they used to share. He always let his boyfriend have a little bit more than him because he knew how much his boyfriend looked forward to it. Then as he goes to turn into the parking lot, some jerk cuts in front of him and makes his bittersweet dairy delight just that bit farther away. What must this girl be thinking, rolling up in her stupid midsize car? Is her nose so stuck up she can't see past it? What an absolute idiot.

So here's to all the people who couldn't wait to get out of their parents' house, only to immediately consider moving back home when they realized they'd have to cook for themselves the rest of their lives. And to the people who get anxiety while engaging in a conference call with more than three people. Let's also hear it for those of us who are certainly capable of walking to the grocery store but would rather just survive on gum. Being a lazy piece of useless will never stop being an option—and a pretty tempting one at that—but you must resist. Like we talked about earlier, you need to get out of your comfort zone. Laziness is a big comfort zone for me. Sitting on the sofa eating jalapeño chips can only do so much damage to my life at the moment. In the long run, however, it makes me unproductive and unenthused about life in general.

So get the hell up and out of the house! Go park in that scary parking lot! When the guy at the stop sign says something mean to you, tune that shit out. You're going to be just fine. Go take on the world confidently. I'm not exactly sure why I should be telling you how to be less of a couch potato, as that's nearly my job, but hey. You're probably missing out on some great adventures in the real world. Even if you get heart palpitations when you see a parking structure.

The Average Grocery List of Eighteen-Year-Old Arden

- two bags of Flamin' Hot Cheetos
- trail mix
- milk
- blue sour straws
- red sour straws
- Fruit by the Foot
- Kraft Singles
- microwavable mac 'n' cheese
- salt-and-vinegar kettle chips
- mayonnaise
- orange juice

CREATING THE PERFECT APARTMENT WITHOUT WADS OF CASH OR BUCKETS OF TEARS

I am a big, big, BIG fan of alone time. Some of you might be surprised to hear that, since I seem like a fairly extroverted and jolly person online. But if someone threatens my relaxation moments, there will be a problem. On multiple occasions I have told people that my apartment was being fumigated just so I didn't have to entertain guests. Some might say that makes me anti-social. I say it makes me attentive to my need for alone time. I spend an absurd number of man-hours carefully cultivating my space when I move to a new apartment. I have to have the right elements come together to create a perfect place of Zen. I would say a pillow isn't out of place by the end of my obsessive decorating, but that's actually the exact opposite of building my ideal home. I have random posters everywhere. There are half-melted candles simmering on every table. Dead or dying flowers can be seen sporadically placed around my apartment. For whatever reason, too many people believe perfection is the key to a comfortable environment. I tend to completely disagree.

Your space should be a reflection of you. Having stark black and whites with marble and gold might feel cool for a little bit, but apartments need to feel lived-in to be cozy. And I'm all about a cozy factor in my living space. Without a feeling of familiarity, a space can feel hollow. Who wants to live in emptiness and overdesign? Not this organizationally challenged lady! Scattered Australian magazines like *Frankie* that I specially order, mismatched blankets pill-y and fluffed out from overuse, and worn-in velvet are just a few of my favorite personal touches. My home is filled with plants in various stages of decay and pinned-up posters from old Japanese movies and video games. My boyfriend, Will, and I strung up our own lighting fixtures and started a rather expansive collection of old books from our individual pasts, coming together to form a perfect literary harmony of graphic novels and soggy romances. Yeah, you could say I'm a quirky individual or whatever. Someone call up Urban Outfitters and let them know I'm down to be a part of their design team if this YouTube thing doesn't work out.

So, no, you don't need to carefully plan out every ounce of your space. In fact, I'd say the more random, the better. Your mind has an odd way of combining looks to make a cohesive whole if you just give it a chance. My apartment is a cluttered mix of past and future Arden colliding at any given time. That means that anything wonderful from my past can be found at hand, be it a picture from my first date with Will, or a ticket stub from that football game I distinctly remember because I threw up in the bathroom during halftime. Ahhh, memories. I'm also constantly rotating in new and fun pieces that have caught my eye or held a special place in my heart. I just bought two graphite drawings at a flea market that were definitely overpriced, but also adorable and relevant to my life. They are now sitting on my countertop, reminding me of running around with my friends trying to haggle vendors while sweating in the blazing heat of downtown LA.

Rule number one in creating a space: only keep the things that you love, but don't be entirely afraid of organized clutter. You can love piles of old cooking books more than the recipes within them. Aesthetic is key. If you want your home to feel like a haven, it needs to feel like it's a part of you. Hang up doodles you've drawn in first period or on a grown-up night in with some friends, and start using ample amounts of Washi tape. That stuff is gold when it comes to taping things up on your walls you don't feel like getting out a hammer and nail for. Absolutely any photo, poster, or paper good that you feel a personal connection with, tack it up on the wall. You'll be surrounded with joyful things whenever you're at home. In my kitchen alone I have a photo collage on my fridge (I know, basic bitch), a collection of birthday cards that Will received from his family on his twenty-third birthday, and the letters A and W carved out of wood sitting above my sink.

Start a collection of some sort. Even if it begins to border on hoarder territory. I have a mug collection like you won't believe. And I LOVE it. It's very cliché of me, but I adore having a specific souvenir with a purpose to bring home from each trip. I always drink tea in the morning, and it's fun to relive memories based on where I purchased each mug. I have some from art collectives in London. I have a couple that Will's mom bought me for Christmas that come with attachments to steep loose-leaf tea. I even have some that I made out of clay candle holders. They tasted a little perfume-y the first few times I used them, and I was probably poisoning myself for a minute there, but those are some of my favorite mugs now. Find out what you use often, and build an army of that object! I also adore pins and patches. Fortunately, they've come back in style as of late, so it's easy to track down cool new ones, but finding vintage or rare accessories is such

a rewarding activity. It doesn't have to be an expensive or taxing hobby. Pick something you'd like to have lying around the house all the time, and make a point to find a cool new addition to your collection when you travel to a unique place.

Someone recently told me that everyone should own a chip-and-dip bowl. You know, one of those modern masterpieces of engineering that allows us to store both chips and various dips in the same receptacle? That way, regardless of how uncool the salsa you bought from Ralphs, you'll always look prepared and efficient. Try to find items for your house that have such enviable dual purposes. I have a small side table in my living room that acts as both a regular old side table and an over-the-couch table for my laptop to rest on instead of my lap. It's changed the game when it comes to doing work while on a very squishy and sloped couch. I love it.

THINGS YOU WILL NEVER FIND IN MY APARTMENT

Bedrooms can be a disaster zone

real quick if you don't allow yourself downtime within them. Make sure you have a desk separate from your bed. Don't email or do work when you're about to go to rest your head on a pillow. Get your lazy ass out of bed and do that stuff at an actual designated work space. If you continue to use your sleep space as a desktop, you're never going to get a good night's rest. Everyone needs separation between work and relaxation. You don't want to become some weird person who ends up sharing a bed with a cup of coffee and a notebook. That's just not a good look for your mental or your heart health. I knew a girl in high school who used her sleep space to get all her work done, and she had perpetual dark circles under her eyes. That could have been due to the fact that she was a workaholic and determined to turn in course work two days early, but I'm fairly certain using a binder as a pillow wasn't helping.

By that same token, spend some time and money cultivating the perfect bed. Maybe that doesn't entail investing in a ten-thousand-dollar Tempur-Pedic mattress, but it does involve lying on a bunch of mattresses to determine your favorite, finding your best thread count, and dropping cash on pillows that make you want to sleep eternally. Not in a sad way, of course. Just in an "if I had to marry one inanimate object in my apartment, it would be my sleeping soul mate, Mr. Down Feather Pillow" kind of way. Once you have all your lovely bed accessories, WASH THEM REGULARLY. Oh my God. I'm talking to my disgusting, naive past self on this one. I would go a full month and a half without washing my sheets. Do you know how much "you" gets trapped in your bed?? So much hair oil. So much dead skin. You could practically make a second human out of all the cells you've been leaving in there. Every week or two, strip your bed and wash it all. The pillows, the sheets. Everything. Trust me, your skin and hair will thank me. It also feels amazing to slide into freshly washed sheets.

And for the love of God, get yourself a good couch. If there's one thing I've learned from sliding off and squishing myself into a scratchy discount couch, it's that I spend too much time on it to not get a nice one next time. I have such resentment toward my couch. It doesn't hug me the right way, it never makes me feel loved. It rejects me nightly when all I want is to feel comfortable in its embrace. I guess it's true what they say: you get what you pay for. And I paid for someone to randomly stab me and silently seethe at me as I attempt to show them affection. I spend a large amount of time chilling in my living room because of my unhealthy addiction to Hulu and Netflix. If I had known the amount of readjusting and tossing and turning I would be doing trying to find a good place to binge-watch shows on my lumpy sofa, I would have invested more money in the damn thing. You can find some truly amazing vintage couches for pretty cheap online. If you find a couch that looks hella comfortable, but is in the grossest stained shape you've ever seen, no worries. There's a simple solution to that. Reupholster! Depending on the size and shape of the couch, nearly any fabric can be ripped off and exchanged for a newer fabric. And it's way cheaper than buying a Swedish designer couch worth more than your actual life. Get yourself a good couch. And if anyone is looking for a gray Ikea love seat at a reasonable price, let me know. Gently used, and slightly demonic, but reasonably priced.

Being picky or having expensive taste in your furniture isn't totally necessary, though. I spent twenty bucks each on my kitchen stools, and they look and feel just fine. Be choosy about the things that really matter (a bed, a couch, and a TV) and let the rest accent the room. Will and I

DIY'd a large portion of our apartment. Everything has a touch of the homemade, since we pretty much re-gig everything we buy. We arranged posters and pictures in our house so they look like they're artfully hanging by twine. We took scraps of newspapers and magazines we liked and displayed them around the apartment. All the flowers that have died in our apartment have culminated in a beautiful bouquet of death that sits right by our window as if to say *Greenery Beware*. We also bought most of our accessories and knickknacks over time rather than buying a large load of junk all at once. It's okay for your house to be sparse for a bit before it feels lived in. No one expects a freshly moved-in human to have an immaculately decorated living space right off the bat. Mine isn't even close to perfect, and I've been living in the same apartment for nearly two years. Take your time, and nurture your home.

I want to stress that your home should be your happy space. If your space is cluttered and messy, your mind will feel cloudy. Make sure you're giving it a light tidy every month or so that includes taking out your vacuum or Swiffer and actually getting rid of the dirt or dust. Even if you clean up after yourself and keep things relatively in order, actual filth builds up without you realizing it. I can't tell you how gross my bathroom had gotten before I had the genius idea to actually buy a mop. It changes the game when your space is so clean you could eat off every surface.

That being said, don't freak out if your home gets a bit messy from time to time. We've all been there. The trash is overflowing. Your floor becomes your closet. You start noticing a bunch of fruit flies everywhere. It's okay. Just take a deep breath (through your mouth), take out the garbage, and relax. You don't need to constantly maintain perfection. That's exhausting, and nobody has time for that kind of self-inflicted worry. If someone asks to come over and you know your apartment looks like a dirty-laundry bomb went off, have them over regardless. People actually don't care. Like, at all. Any time I go over to someone else's place and it's a slight mess, I feel more

at ease. This person is a human being with more important things going on in their lives than constantly worrying
about cleaning every visible surface. Just like me! Obviously you shouldn't strive to have a pigpen of a home, but
it's good to give yourself a well-deserved cleaning break
every now and then, and not feel guilty about it.

If I'm really feeling like treating myself on a special
occasion, I'll hire a cleaning service. I know that sounds
like I'm the queen of France, but it can be cheaper than
you think. When I have a particularly stressful month, or
I know that my space needs to be completely cleaned top

to bottom, for sixty bucks I can have someone do it for me. The idea of coming home to a completely spotless apartment that I didn't have to get on my hands and knees to clean is my fantasy. I've only had my place cleaned professionally twice, but man oh man does it make you envy über-rich people who have a cleaning lady on retainer. Save up a little extra to get your house cleaned, and treat yourself on a special occasion. Trust me, it's worth it.

In short, when someone walks into your living quarters, you want them to know who lives there. That doesn't mean you have to spend large sums of money to get one-of-a-kind furniture or art specifically tailored to your personality. Screw that nonsense and save it for when you get stupid rich. Until then, just make sure that your own personal touches can be seen throughout your home. Buy that weird pug doily that you found at a thrift store for two dollars and turn it into a coaster. Make use of Craigslist. There are too many vintage armchairs and velvet lovelies in need of a home on that site. Get creative and look for ways to turn the ordinary on its head.

Buy plants. Buy all the plants in the whole wide world. The amount of greenery in my home is borderline concerning, but I can't tell you how relaxing and pleasant it is to have little flora friends hanging out with me all the time. If you're anything like me and you kill plants just by looking in their general direction, invest in succulents. You can get adorable teeny cacti that fit perfectly in close-quarter dorm rooms, or you can get big mama aloe veras to hang out in the corner of your two-bedroom apartment. Plants are cheap, cute as hell, and they are scientifically proven to brighten your mood. Take a weekend and go wander around your local farmers' market or plant nursery. You'll take home so many beautiful plant friends you won't even know what to do with them! Just make sure to check with the seller and ask about watering schedules and sunlight needs. Some plants need direct sunlight with only minimal watering, while others will die after just a day without water. Take care of the little guys. They're a great tester to see if you can handle even the lowest maintenance pet!

If you live in more *ahem* minimalist quarters (I'm talking dorm rooms, studio apartments, etc.), make the most of the space you have. I have seen some incredible feats of human ingenuity when it comes to the task of making a space multipurpose. I've seen people with beds that retract from cabinets. I love the idea of using a projector instead of a TV to save room. Get resourceful. My sister MacGyver'ed her bed with her roommates and made a ramshackle bunk bed so they could have extra living space in their dorm room. They then hid both of their desks on either side of the bed tower to save additional wall space. Ahh, the resourcefulness of cramped college students! Take a page from my sister's book and don't be afraid to stick some duct tape on an idea and call it genius.

I need me-time, and I only can spend me-time in a place tailored for . . . me. My space is where I regenerate, it's where I learn, and it's where I relax. I need it to fulfill all those requirements and also be a harbor for all my favorite items and memories. When I come home from a long day of social obligations or work, I want to feel at ease and relaxed. I want to enter my home and feel the snug warmth of familiarity when I get the first whiff of my apartment's particular scent. Never settle for an unsatisfactory living space. Make a point to morph it over time into something you're proud of. You can make something feel like home regardless of budget. Just don't skimp on a couch. Trust me on that one. It's not worth the heartbreak or the chiropractor bill.

Cool Things to Have Lying Around Your Home

- Vintage magazines with interesting covers
- A collection of your favorite records readily available to play
- Candles. Everywhere.
- Duct tape
- Plants! Preferably ones that don't die easily.
- A couple of card games that are good in a pinch!
- Coasters everywhere
- Zip ties
- Cozy blankets and a basket to organize them in
- Chloroform

FINDING A DECENT DATE IN AN ONLINE WORLD

'm going to be honest with you: I don't love modern dating apps. My six-month stint browsing Tinder gave me enough reasons to hate the entire practice of finding a suitable date from a bio and a blurry selfie taken two years ago at Coachella. I feel like using an app to find dates is a skill honed and perfected over time. Users who have been active members for longer seem to get more dates, more quickly. The act of getting a date with someone feels like a video game with an incredibly competitive stat board. It seems to go against my entire conception of a dating app: finding "the One" in a genuine and honest place. In my life, I would use Tinder to scan potential date options and find someone I could actually see myself going out with. I know from friends that other people are just trying to find hookups or, in many cases, one-night stands.

There's no way to figure out on the app what someone's intentions are before you actually sit down with them and have a conversation. They might say they want a long-term relationship in their bio, but I'm sure many have learned that the guise of commitment can get you more dates. And you can change your profile picture until you harbor enough data to determine which selfie gets you the most swipes. There are in-depth and lengthy articles online discussing the best words and quirky phrases to use in your bio. Being humble, funny, and extremely good-looking can be a surprisingly easy triathlon to perform when you have complete control over your image. Obviously it only takes one real conversation to rule out a person if they're suspicious, but it's crazy that you could fall in love with the "appearance" of someone and then learn that they are a completely different person.

Most people on dating apps are there to confront some kind of boredom. Sexual boredom seems to be the main driving force behind male participation (the number of unsolicited shirtless selfies women are subjected to on a regular basis seems to be a testament to that notion). When talking to girls I know who regularly use these apps, they all seem to enjoy playing these desperate men like a game, intent on boosting their own self-esteem. They'll regale me in great detail with the number of y's trailing the end of "heys" they receive from interested guys. And then, flicking through the bathing-suit pool pics a potential date sent when asked what he was up to, they'll giddily announce that he didn't even ask her what she was wearing or what she was up to that same night! What a catch! The more simultaneously attractive and normal the dude seems by the end of this fifteen-minute exchange, the more of a win on the girl's part.

It's easy to find eccentric and slightly offensive people on dating apps—it's a more challenging task to find someone who shares the same values as you. It takes some digging to get past the undesirables. All I really wanted in dating apps was to find someone who would sit and watch Netflix with me without making a sexist or derogatory comment every couple minutes. It's hard to find men on dating apps who don't immediately want to show you their genitals. Most of the time, bad Tinder dates end with the lasting enjoyment of a well-rounded story to tell. That's the main benefit of dating an endless stream of unsatisfactory people. You get to complain about the horrible event to your friends afterward. You might have gone on a date with someone on a government watch list without knowing it. Or someone who married his cousin by mistake a couple years ago. Although the interaction may end on a positive note, this nearly never continues with a second date. Girls continue to riffle through various guys, not unlike a new special on the Cheesecake Factory menu. Maybe something interesting for a moment, but only to be savored for a limited amount of time. God forbid someone actually meets their lasting final love ONLINE.

I know you probably think I'm a cynical jerk who hates online dating because I had a few bad matches on Tinder. But that couldn't be further from the truth. I love meeting new people online. It's how I came to be dating my boyfriend right now.

Actually, I also have Rebecca Black to thank. I know that sounds like the most obnoxiously internet thing for me to say, but let me walk it back and explain how this all came to pass.

I was waiting in line for a drink at one of the many overly crowded after-parties featured at VidCon. VidCon (for those of you who aren't hip, up-to-date millennials) is a YouTube convention that happens once a year in Anaheim, California, where internet personalities flock from all over to meet hundreds of their most loyal viewers. At this particular VidCon, I was dating someone I was rapidly falling out of love with, and I was on the edge of breaking up with him nearly every time we spoke.

I was standing in this drink line, and a giraffe-like

acquaintance of mine was chattering on behind me while we both endured the agonizing twenty-five-minute wait for a Diet Coke. I'd occasionally look back to make a funny remark or make sure he hadn't abandoned me for a superior drink line with a shorter wait time. But there he remained, stuck right at my rear for the nearly half hour of agony. He was a nice guy, but at a certain point, I was pretty done with drink-line talk. You can only repeat how well your night's going three times before you start worrying your line buddy has short-term memory issues. So, in one final show of separation, I decided to turn around and give him a big smile and say something along the lines of, "Jeez, better give the ladies behind you some attention" to get him off my butt. But as I turned around to finish the end of my quip, I realized that my partner in line crime had abandoned me and a new giraffe had taken his place.

"Sorry? Were you talking to me?" A rather confused-sounding British accent lilted into my ears as I realized in horror that I was staring at dimples that could melt even the iciest of hearts. Two very befuddled blue eyes looked down on me worriedly. I don't even want to think about how I must have seemed, telling him to go conversate with the other ladies when we hadn't even made eye contact! So if you were wondering, now you know: I'm so smooth you could use my moves to ice a wedding cake. Stunned, and more than a bit embarrassed, I called him by the name of my (traitorous) ex–line buddy. He assured me that he wasn't a shape-shifter and introduced himself as Will Darbyshire.

Helloooo, Mr. Darbyshire. Unbeknownst to me, Will was also in a (lackluster) relationship at the time, so our timing was astronomically off. Both of us were at the end of the line in our current relationships, but we also weren't cheating scumbags. We made casual, emphatically non-romantic small talk for the remaining ten minutes of line time, and then we said our good-byes and went off into our separate evenings. I had a feeling this was an introduction I would remember, and I had clocked the way he looked at me, but I had also already finished my Diet Coke and I was already looking for a new line partner to take me through another arduous journey.

But my and Will's story didn't end there. I broke up with my boyfriend about a month after VidCon ended. I cried about it nearly every night for the following three months. My ex had been my first real boyfriend. He had followed me from high school to my move to California, and he felt like my connection to Arkansas. I felt like someone had cut my safety net in half. Ultimately I know my young self made the right choice, but I regretted my decision for months. I spent my morning showers crying. I ate Chipotle crying. I watched *New Girl* crying. It was a very wet and snotty time. I didn't know the human body was capable of excreting that much liquid. I felt like at any second I was going to hit full raisin mode, totally devoid of any fluids left to weep out. But lo and behold, every time I thought the sobs were subsiding, they resurfaced stronger than ever at any mention of my former lover. This was usually when I played a video game I'd last played with my ex, or when a Blink-182 song came on in a store (yeah, we were THAT couple in high school). I have a specific memory of bursting into tears while walking through the underwear aisle of Target as "First Date" faintly echoed throughout the clothing department. Such a mess. And not a hot one.

This kind of tragic self-pity went on for a long, solid while. Probably a little too long for my own good. During that time I went on a grand total of three dates. One was with a guy who didn't think we were on a date. We ate tomato soup. Another one was at a party with a beautiful Greek man. It wasn't really a date, but I want to count it since it was the closest thing I came to hooking up with someone while I was single, and he had a man bun. The third date was with a thirty-one-year-old British man who drove a Porsche. I was nineteen at the time.

I had begun to get desperate.

During this bizarro period of semi-dates, I started noticing that one William Darbyshire had been tweeting at me. He would randomly tell me I looked beautiful if I posted a selfie. Or he would reply to a funny tweet of mine with a well-placed emoji (no big, I'm hilarious online). It wasn't a disturbing number of tweets, but being the extra-sensitive narcissist that I am, I began to get creeped out. Not because anything he did warranted a *To Catch a Predator* moment, but because I hadn't ever had a guy online treat me as if I was worthy of praise like he did. He was outright. He didn't care that I wasn't responding. He kept sending me pleasantries and small flatteries. It was sorta cute. But also creepy to me. Mainly because I HAD FORGOTTEN I HAD ALREADY MET HIM. I'm the worst. I kept wondering who this mysterious man was. What did he sound like? How tall was he? My stupid brain didn't register that I already knew what he sounded and looked like. I went on like this, passively checking in to see if he had said anything new to me online, until I finally had enough curiosity to ask a friend about him. I was sitting in the kitchen with Jenn and Lauren (roommates and YouTubers extraordinaire) when someone rang the doorbell.

Jenn popped downstairs and reappeared moments later with Rebecca Black. After making small talk for a good bit, we all got onto participating in one of our favorite activities: talking absolute shit. Now I'm not saying we were huge gossips. But we were huge gossips whenever we gathered in the kitchen. It was rarely a negative conversation; it usually went something like this:

"Wait, those two are dating now? I thought she was dating a Mormon from Detroit."

"No, they broke up three weeks ago. He's with that girl who hosts Radio Disney events."

Nothing overtly harmful was ever discussed during our sessions, but on this night in particular, I had some questions for Ms. Black. I knew she had a tentative connection to Will, and I wanted the dirt on what his deal was. When I showed her the tweets and voiced my concern at the forwardness of this internet stranger, Rebecca freaked out. "You don't know Will?! How do you not know Will!! You guys would be soooo perfect for each other! He's so sweet and kind and gentle and wonderful and probably is a really good kisser and he has a British accent and he treats girls really nicely I bet and—"

She might not have actually said the entirety of that rant, but the feeling I got after finishing a long chat with her was that I would be stupid not to at least give him a chance. So I messaged him. And we chatted. And he seemed like a normal person. No psychopathic tendencies or hints of craziness. Just a nice, normal man. Exactly what I was looking for during my lackluster Tinder swiping sessions. So I gave him my number and told him that we should hang out next time he was in LA. He was living in London, but he made the trip out to LA on a regular basis for work or to visit friends. About a month after our chat conversation, I received a mysterious text message. All it said was,

Hey! It's Will! I'm going to be in town next week
if you want to meet up :)

I replied,

Oh my God Will! I haven't seen you in so long.

It'll be nice to see a hometown friend in Cali for once :)

I thought Will was a Will who I had grown up with in Arkansas. Hometown Will had a brother going to college in Malibu, and I assumed he would be a Will who would visit the West Coast occasionally. I had saved neither hometown nor London Will's number, and it was just a matter of time before that switch-up complicated things.

Ha-ha what? Sorry, this is Will from London. LOL.

Hah. This was embarrassing. I closed the message and pretended it hadn't happened. I didn't text him back. I told myself I would, but I didn't. I think I was a bit ashamed of looking like such an idiot, but I mainly didn't know if I was ready to hang out with this Will. I was still in my "are these tears or shower water" phase of relationship grief, and I wasn't sure if I could move on with my romantic life just yet. Ending a three-year relationship was pretty tough. And this man was British and cute. I had convinced myself that rejection was inevitable. We would go on one date, I would act like a weirdo, and he wouldn't get that my whole thing was being a weirdo.

So I went ice cold. I didn't reply to his message, and I'm pretty sure he thought my cell phone had self-destructed or something. He wrote me on Twitter later that week reaffirming that he'd sent me a text and would be so happy if he could see me when he was in town. Being the impulsive people pleaser I was, I said yes. Hesitantly. Obviously he didn't know what a melty, sobbing mess I was on the other side of that Twitter profile, and he set us up to have a coffee shop date on Melrose. How charming of him, damn it! Getting ready for the date, I cried. I cried when I picked out my outfit. I cried when I turned on my shower faucet. I cried when I washed the shampoo out of my hair. I cried when I toweled off. I cried when I texted him to cancel our date because I was crying so much.

Will had already been at the coffee shop waiting for me for an hour. I know this now because he bitterly retold his side of the story after we had been dating for about four months. Will thought I was just a flighty turd after that. But he still had a crush. I think I stuck in the back of his head for a while since I was so damn hard to pin down. Such was the life of someone pining after an emotionally unavailable asshat like myself. Poor guy.

Will and I easily could have met up that day and had coffee and talked to each other and laughed and then hugged good-bye and never dated each other ever again; I was in a weird place at that time, and so was he. Our timing wasn't great during coffee time, just like it wasn't great when we met in the drinks line. Beverages should never have been involved in the genesis of our relationship. It wasn't until January 2015 that we went on our first real date. Since June we had been ships passing in the night, always just missing each other. It took six months for us to finally find a place we could meet.

I had rented out an apartment in London for two weeks at the beginning of January. My friend Cat had asked me months prior if I was down to go on a European excursion and I, being the impulsive creature I am, said yes. We ended up booking everything only a couple weeks before leaving. During this time, I was heavily Snapchatting and sliding into Will's DMs. After what Rebecca had said and what I had discovered when I finally checked out his YouTube, I knew Will to be an extremely interesting guy. The videos he produced on his channel were beautiful short films highlighting different elements in his life. He would spend weeks on each one, carefully articulating his thoughts about the world while maintaining the goofy quirkiness that had instantly drawn me in. He didn't like being on camera, and there was something adorable about his awkwardness. One of the first videos of his I ever watched was "A Letter to My Future Wife." It was during the last five sec-onds of that video, as I processed finally hearing his voice and looking through the glasses through which he saw the world, that I realized I needed to get up on Mr. Darbyshire or I was making a huge mistake. I wanted to do more than text him

occasionally about the new *Game of Thrones* episode. So we made a real date. I was going to be in London. He was picking me up at my rented apartment in West Hempstead. He had my address. This was the point of no return. Either I went on this date, or I would have to fake my own death.

He showed up at my door a bit late. The apartment I was staying in had a secondary door at the bottom of a long set of stairs that led outside. That door was already open by the time I had exited the actual apartment. He was standing there, at the base of the stairs, looking adorably bundled up. Since it was freezing outside, he was in a long black wool coat with a gray lined collar, a pill-y sweater peeking out from behind a knitted scarf cozily coiled around his neck. He was past six feet tall, but from my vantage point up the stairs he looked like a well-dressed, dimpled, bespectacled man of a reasonable height. It wasn't until I began descending the stairs toward him that a fun-house-mirror moment happened and I remembered being a good eleven inches shorter than my towering date. It was superhot. Not gonna lie.

We walked to dinner. He took me on the Tube for the first time and helped me buy a ticket. While walking through the hectic crisscross streets of central London, I had a hard time discerning the direction traffic was coming from. I had a couple near-death experiences, since I was focusing so hard on Will's face. I stepped too confidently out onto the road right as a bus was making a turn around the corner. In my Yankee head, I assumed it was going to turn. It was not. Will wrapped one of his Gumby arms around my waist and firmly but gently pulled me back to safety. In that moment, I knew I was going to kiss all up on his face later that night.

Will and I have been dating since then. And I 100 percent have the internet to thank for bringing us together. From the people online like Rebecca, to the apps in which we connected, the internet afforded Will and me the opportunity to have a relationship. Because we spent so much of our time trying to come up with things to chat about, we ended up knowing everything about the other person by the time we met in the real world. It was like we had a relationship already built and ready to move into once we could actually be physically together. We had spent so much time guessing what the other person was going to be like in the flesh, when in reality, we already knew. We had spent a large portion of time studying the words and thoughts of each other without even realizing it. We didn't meet on Tinder or Bumble or Hinge or any other one-word dating app, but we were as millennial as it gets. One of our first interactions was a tweet. We Snapchatted each other for a month before meeting for our first date in real life. Even though we were on two different sides of the world, we were lucky to be born into and live in a time where that kind of separation didn't mean our relationship was inconceivable.

And that's why I advocate meeting your significant other online. App, website, forum, message board, social media—doesn't matter. Even if I think Tinder can be silly and vapid at times. Even if you have to vet people through your friends with more scrutiny. Because, really, how likely are you to bump into your soul mate in real life? ("But, Arden, you literally bumped into Will in a line at Vid—" Shhhhhhhhh.) With seven billion people wandering around the planet, I'd say it's a good idea to explore more dating opportunities than just your next-door neighbor. "Don't talk to strangers online" has become an archaic piece of advice that simply doesn't apply to our oversharing generation of supersleuths. With the right level of judgment and discernment, you can find a best friend, or a boyfriend, without ever leaving your bedroom.

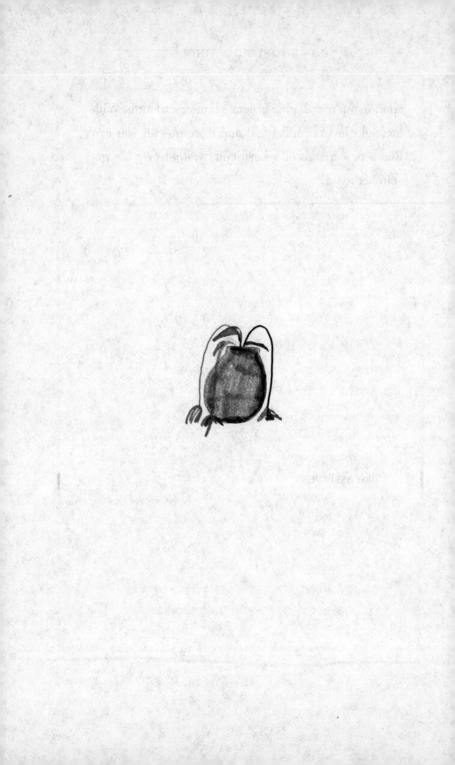

Checklist for the Perfect
Boyfriend or Girlfriend

☐ A connection that feels truly in sync.

☐ The ability to set aside personal gratification in an argument, to cool down and discuss issues like adults.

☐ Really great back-scratching/rubbing technique.

☐ An open recognition of others' attractiveness. If a guy can't admit that Ryan Gosling can get it, he's a liar. And I don't date liars. Or homophobes.

☐ An understanding that people make mistakes in life. We're all just humans with innately selfish intentions trying to do our best not to act like assholes.

☐ Will sacrifice the first sip of a water bottle or the last sour gummy worm in the bag at any request.

☐ Will make sure to ask you if you're hot or cold at any given time. Also willing to hold or give up a jacket when the temperature calls for it.

THAT TIME I LITERALLY STARTED PULLING OUT MY HAIR

Every time I heard about obsessive-compulsive disorder when I was little, it was people complaining about how crooked picture frames or mismatched pillowcases made them irritable. No one really mentioned the stress of feeling like you might burn down your house if you didn't check the stove three times before leaving. And no one told me that picking at your hair or your skin until you bled fell somewhere along the OCD spectrum, either. It wasn't until I had pulled out all my eyelashes and eyebrows at thirteen years old that I thought I might have a *slight* issue that needed tending to.

I have trichotillomania and it has me. Trich is defined as a compulsive need to pick out or pull one's hair. It's a disorder that is common in young children but usually gets sorted out in adolescence. Unfortunately, my trich wasn't having that. I was a carefree, long-lashed baby face until I hit my teen years. I wasn't an immediately stressed out and anxious teenager, but I would have days that felt like a lot of work. At the end of a long day, all I wanted was something to make me feel calm and comforted. For whatever reason, I was wired to find relaxation in pulling out my hair. At the beginning of arguably the worst four years of self-consciousness and peer-to-peer image shaming (aka high school), the urge to pick out my eyelashes and eyebrows surfaced.

It started off as a harmless way to unwind at the end of the day. I had just recently begun to wear light traces of makeup. During the day I would apply a bit of foundation and some mascara, which would inevitably come off at night before bed. Instead of just using a cleanser or makeup wipe to get rid of my mascara, I started pulling the clumps off my lashes. I thought I was merely getting my makeup off. But then I began to feel an odd satisfaction anytime I pulled. It became a ritual in which I would apply a crazy amount of mascara, let it dry for a couple of minutes, and then excitedly rip it all off once it hardened. The cakier and more spidery the better! Eventually I realized that I didn't have to constantly layer coat after coat to get the same satisfaction I craved. I could just pull out my eyelashes.

It wasn't like I sat down and decided to perform this really odd ritual every day. It just became a thing of habit. Anytime I was tired or stressed out, it was my go-to activity to help my mind zone out. I would pick before bed. I would pick right when my alarm went off in the morning. I would pick when I was hungry. I would pick doing homework. It got to the point where I had to start picking at my eyebrows because my eyelids were all but barren of lashes. I spent an entire summer feeding my new compulsion, and it made me look a bit alien by the end of it all. It never hurt, by the way. Sometimes my eyelids or eyebrows might be sore, but it was never really painful. By the time I was deep into my trich, I didn't feel a thing when I pulled because my face was scarred.

I strolled up to my first day of freshman year of high

school with carefully etched-in eyebrows and a cover-all coat of eyeliner. Up close, you could see something was slightly off with my face, so I avoided intimate conversations. I wore makeup every single day of school from fourteen to sixteen. Same eyeliner. Same obviously artificial eyebrows. I don't think anyone ever knew exactly what I looked like under all of it, but a few people certainly were overly curious about my facade. I would touch up after class if I slipped and pulled during a long, monotonous lecture or overly stressful exam. I think some of my friends noticed my problem, but none of them ever said anything about it, and I never came right out and said I was struggling. I felt like I had a secret that was made public every time my makeup wore off.

It wasn't until one afternoon at cheer practice in the dead of summer before my sophomore year that someone finally called me out. The team had to complete rigorous exercises in a relatively short amount of time, being expected to run, sweat, and run some more. That meant an hour of intensive sweating with no room for a makeup touch-up. I prayed to God my mask hadn't melted. We ended this practice with a quick powwow before any bathroom breaks could be taken. Unbeknownst to me, my eyebrows had become my eyeliner, and my eyeliner had become my under-eyeliner. My entire face had shifted downward, leaving my bare brow bone exposed.

Being the unaware, unintentional asshole that a teen girl can be, one of my teammates sat down cross-legged next to me to stare at my face. She asked me where my eyebrows had gone. I told her I had picked them out. She asked me why I would do that. I told her to go to hell.

Okay, that's not quite how it went. I really wish I had been secure enough in myself at sixteen to actually tell her something along those lines. Sadly, instead I resorted to mumbling something about OCD and pretending I was tired out from practice so that I could hide my screwed-up face under the shade of my arm.

I went on like that in a constant state of fear of discovery, and subsequent shame, for most of my adolescence. I didn't want anyone to see me as bizarre or disturbed. I couldn't stop what I was doing to my face, but I also couldn't handle the critique when someone caught me. It's not like I wanted to pick—I just felt so much better after I did. But I also felt terrible when I saw the repercussions right on my face. It was a vicious cycle where I would feel insecure and down, so I would pick to feel better. Then once I had gone through my ritual and felt mentally better, I wrecked my face and didn't feel great about it anymore. I wanted to stop so badly, but I had no one telling me how to snap out of it. It was such a rare issue and something that didn't have an actual cure. I felt hopeless for a long while.

As I grew older and accepted my face sans hair, it got easier to explain my disorder. Fortunately, I had a fairly forgiving school that wasn't prone to all-out bullying people. My classmates generally let me be and only occasionally asked questions when their curiosity got the best of them. For the most part, I was able to come to terms with my issues in my own time. One school night, I had gone on a picking binge in bed and didn't check what I looked like before I left the house the next morning for school. After first period, I went to go check in the bathroom to assess the damage, and I realized that I had absolutely no eyebrows. I had gone a whole class period without them. I fumbled around in my purse and found a dark chocolate colored liquid eyeliner that I attempted to fashion into eyebrows. I looked like I had taken a brown Sharpie to my eyes. At first I wanted to cry and sneak out of school and drive into a lake or something. But then I decided to just say fuck it and go on with my day, business as usual. No one actually cared what my face looked like, and if they did, they never mentioned it to me.

It took me a good four years to accept that I had a problem that couldn't be solved with a pill or a therapist. Trich can be managed, but not cured. I'm currently in remission, meaning I don't feel a strong urge to pick, and I attribute it entirely to the fact that I've stopped letting myself feel shame. I'm no longer looking for an excuse or crutch to lean on and help me. Every-thing that was supposed to cure me just made me disappointed and desperate. I now know the only thing I can do to save myself from a spiral is being confident in the fact that I will never have it completely under control, and that's totally fine.

So much of having a disorder is living in shame. Shame of being caught, shame of being seen looking different from others, and shame of having to take complete responsibility for what you've done. Once I stopped seeing myself as a breakdown waiting to happen, I started feeling more in control. I thought of my problem as a work in progress, not a disaster that I'd been left with to handle. I was gentler with my mental health, and I found a community online that made my disorder feel relatively normal. I was no longer the only one I knew dealing with this. There were other girls and guys out there with bald scalps and bleeding follicles. I could relate to and understand them, and I could also recognize they were in bad, dark places I didn't want to reach. It made me realize how fortunate I was that I could successfully conceal my missing facial features. These online friends forced me to stop feeling like I needed to hide.

In LA I started going to the grocery store or my local coffee shop without any makeup on. The general public saw my worst and never said a thing. Once, I went to Chipotle, and as I was going through the order line, I realized one of the employees had no eyelashes or eyebrows. As

I was checking out, I plucked up the courage to ask if it was trich. She said yes and seemed shocked that I knew what the disorder entailed. I explained that I had been suffering from it for years, and all she could ask was how I had beaten it. I looked like someone who had conquered trich! What a boost of confidence that was! I wished her the best of luck and she gave me free guacamole. What a cool girl.

All my nightmares of public shaming were unsubstantiated. If anything, I had several kindred spirits come up to me and gently commend me for showing face when they didn't feel comfortable doing so. It was surprisingly helpful for my self-esteem. I made a video online talking about my trich and had even more people flocking to the comments to share their own struggles with OCD and impulse control disorder.

Disorders make you feel like you're singled out and shoved in an unwanted spotlight. You want to hide and you want to ignore your issues while still allowing them to manifest. But telling people and being forthright with a deep-rooted problem is the best cure for any mental illness you have. Create a circle of helpers around you who can keep you in a positive upswing and help you when you dip low. Without a support system, even the strongest of individuals can crumble. Talk about it when you're not doing well. Celebrate when you're at your best. Make sure everyone around you is on the same page when it comes to your triggers.

BRAIN

I have to give a special thank-you to Will for always holding my hand or letting me pick at his back when I'm feeling stressed out or like I want to pull. He's been the absolute standard for a person with a significant other with mental health issues. Will's undeniably the number-one person who's kept me solid and firm in my recovery.

No other person, doctor, or therapist has made such a positive impact on my trich. I hope to anyone out there who's struggling with a similar issue that you find your William one day. Or learn how to be one yourself for others.

SOMEONE ACTUALLY
ADVOCATING LONG DISTANCE

People used to have such limited resources to fall in love with someone else. Just take a look at the rate at which marrying your first cousin has gone out of style and you'll see how much choice we have now! As I have already made clear, I think the gift of technology is a blessing in the game of modern romance. But, as with most things, there's a dark side to it, too. Anyone with a smartphone and a witty caption in their dating profile can take their pick of the throngs of desperate individuals. Because we now have the luxury of choice factored into finding our soul mate, we've become a picky, lonely generation. Height, religion, and a preference or distaste for sushi can all be valid reasons not to give someone a chance.

Online dating is becoming the standard in finding a partner. As I mentioned, I met my own boyfriend online. We've gone from being tirelessly reminded to "not talk to strangers online" to being forced to talk to randoms online every day. I can honestly say most of my intimate relationships operate on the internet. Granted, I work on YouTube, which has resulted in my personal life being a much more public life online, but I think that this is becoming the norm for everyone else as well. Will has a group of girls who religiously follow him online and share a chat on Twitter with him, where he occasionally checks in to see how they're getting on with their lives. He's not looming over them creepily, but they have really funny conversations about the goings-on of the YouTube world and ask for his insight or opinions about internet gossip. The chat is just best girlfriends gabbing endlessly (as only teenage girls can)—it looks exactly like how my hometown friends and I used to text. It's familiar and safe. Secrets are revealed. Double-chin selfies are unabashedly shared. The word "slay" is used a lot. And yet, most of these girls have never met in person. Some of them live in Auckland, New Zealand, some of them live in more remote portions of the country, and I think one of them lives in Australia. Yet they all have a bond like their mothers gave birth right next to each other.

I read a study a couple years ago concluding that people can't tell the difference between friends they meet online and in person. You can make the same emotional interpersonal connection on the internet that you can make with your next-door neighbor. This is absolutely amazing to me. It means that you can find your people, your tribe, online. It doesn't matter what you're into, you can find someone who feels the same way about dressing up in animal costumes and having group sex together. Yay internet! This is especially helpful if you're anything like me and curdle at the idea of meeting . . . New People.

I'm sort of kidding, but I'm also not. I find it hard to make deep connections with people. I like meeting people casually at parties; I love a good party friend. But the moment someone gets out their Oprah face and tries to dig into my soul, I immediately scuttle into the corner of my brain far away from all in-depth conversations. The opposite is true when I'm chatting with someone online.

I know that sounds crazy, but I find it easier to be honest and forthright with my opinions when I have a computer to hide behind. I'm like an emotional troll. I might not spew hate-speech, but I will endlessly ramble about why I think virginity is stupid or how dumb it is that women have to pay for tampons. Being able to have a second to articulate my feelings or thoughts is reassuring in a weird way. I find that I like meeting people online. I like having a casual Twitter chat turn into Snapchatting. And then Snapchatting turning into Skyping. And then Skyping turning into a week in London turning into a two-year relationship! There's a clearly defined stepladder of comfort that I ascended while dating Will. (Little did I know I would need the same ladder to kiss him when I realized he wasn't joking about being six-four.) I had a good sense that this gangly, mop-haired British guy was going to make me a cup of tea every morning.

So you fell in love with someone out of physical reach. This results in lots of lackluster Wi-Fi connections while trying to have meaningful bonding experiences over FaceTime. The ability to talk and see someone continents away is staggering, true, but Skype and FaceTime suck ass once you begin to rely on them to make your relationship work. I can't tell you how many solid thirty-minute blocks Will and I have spent trying to get past the laws of physics to teleport. In a way, the challenges of long-distance relationships are some of the most reward-ing. You both think of each other hundreds of miles away, and there's something utterly lonesome about the whole thing. But there's also a sense of comfort that comes with two people on the same level of pining after one another. Each person knows without a shadow of a doubt that their lives are going to get significantly better once they see the other person. It's hard to commit to that lonely ordeal without a damn good thing waiting for you on the other side, but when there is, it's worth it. You spend so much of your time together just appreciating the pres-ence of the other person. You can touch and feel and be with them as much as you want for a short period of time before you have to take those same memories of close-ness with you on a plane ride ten hours away. You learn to appreciate every moment with your significant other. You also spend so much time talking about all the things you'll be able to do once you're together. I remember my first trip to London to visit Will like it was yesterday. We had planned out museum tours and shopping and dinners and drinks. We would get so excited about all the fun activities we could enjoy together. It's an anticipation that makes it all the better when you finally get to see that person.

I'd like to repeat that this can and does apply to platonic friendships as well. I've been to a couple VidCons in my time, and I can't tell you how often I've seen groups of people who are meeting in real life for the first time. I remember two girls with brightly colored hair in line for a meet-up telling me they'd been friends for three years but had just met in person that morning. I wondered if they shared an intense feeling that moment they heard their actual voices, unaltered by the robotic tone of a webcam. As they tucked into Starbucks croissants, did they feel validated by their choice to commit to someone they would rarely be in physical contact with? Or did they just start chatting it up with each other, business as usual? They had shared a personal connection for three years with another human without ever touching them—or knowing how tall they really were. Crazy.

So I 100 percent support talking to strangers online. As long as they're not catfishing you or trying to sell you meth. The good thing is, you can spot fake profiles incredibly easily nowadays. Do they have more than ten friends on Facebook? Great! Do those friends have posts and activity on their Facebook? Perfect. They're probably a real person. If they don't have any other forms of social media, or don't have friends connected to their profiles, those are all red flags for fake profiles. I wish I had really leaned into meeting friends online in high school. I lost a good chunk of my friend group due to pettiness and being a teenager, and I felt incredibly isolated when I was younger. Seeing all these girls supporting one another and finding true lasting friendships online makes me feel so glad for them, but it also gives me a twinge of missed opportunity. If you ever feel like you don't fit in, or you aren't connected with the people directly in contact with you in the real world, find your people online—either romantically, or with solid friendships.

Anyone currently in a long-distance relationship can probably relate to my duality of feelings toward airports. I hate airports. But I also love them dearly and feel like LAX is my second home. At this point, they should give me an honorary wing in Terminal 2. It would just be a room with a bed, mini toothbrush, airplane-friendly versions of my favorite skin care, and a whole bunch of prepackaged snacks that won't make me gassy on a ten-hour flight. I can't tell you how many times rose-hip oil and Soap & Glory face wipes have saved my life on long plane flights. My skin tends to become a disaster zone if I plan on spending more than five hours in the sky, so I take off all my makeup and douse my skin in oil. It creates a protective moisturized layer that helps prevent breakouts. Pro tip for that superlong flight between you and your prospective friend/lover: bring snacks, two books, and a laptop loaded with a new TV show you've been meaning to binge to distract you from your nerves. I've gotten to the point where I've watched all the new movies and shows that you can watch on a plane's built-in entertainment center, and the influx of new content is never big enough to keep me preoccupied for more than a couple hours. You can only watch the same episodes of *New Girl* so many times. I've had to take my entertainment into my own hands.

Ultimately, the irritating game of endurance required in long-distance relationships is nearly always worth it. If it weren't, you wouldn't still be talking to that person you've chosen to invest so much time in. You know you truly care about them when you'll forgo the constant assurance of physical closeness. I'll gladly sacrifice a few weeks to impatience and loneliness to date my boyfriend. And that's how I know I love him. All the aches and pains of being apart from someone are a testament to how much you do want to be with them. As I'm typing this, Will is in London, and I'm in a café in LA, overly caffeinated and antsy. We're going to see each other again in nine days. And I'm so unbelievably excited. I can't wait for him to see my new haircut. I can't wait to hug his leg. I can't wait to snuggle up and take a nap with him. And all of these things are reasons why it's okay that we have to be apart for a little while. We both know it's necessary to be apart so we can be together.

If you've ever thought about dating someone or making a new friend online only to stop yourself because you'd be limited to Skype calls and text messages in different time zones, reconsider. Our world is rapidly adapting to the internet. We're all becoming more connected. Transportation is only going to get better. FaceTime connections will (hopefully) only improve. We now have a way to actively combat loneliness and isolation. Give an internet relationship a chance. Trust me, it'll be worth it. As long as you're not giving out your social security number, or posting your address as your Twitter bio.

Things to Do in Any Domestic Row

- Stay above petty criticism.
- Try to understand the other person's side.
- Forgo your pride when you see an opportunity for reconciliation.
- Keep your voice at a reasonable decibel level.
- Specify how the situation makes you feel rather than blaming the other person.
- Leave the past in the past.

Things Not to Do in Any Domestic Row

- Call the other person a selfish dick.

THE MOMENT I REALIZED THAT I
WAS A GROWN-ASS WOMAN

'm going to tell you the truth: Most adults don't feel like adults. I'm technically of adulting age, and I still feel like I shouldn't be allowed in R-rated movies without a legal guardian. Truth be told, there isn't a day when your application is accepted. There isn't an "aha!" moment when you realize you've finally passed the threshold into adulthood. You don't lean back in a La-Z-Boy after hours of doing taxes and reviewing your retirement options and think, "Here I am. I've made it. My youth has been thoroughly spent." Becoming an adult is more like a series of "Oh crap" moments that make you realize you've been adulting it all along. Most of the time you stumble into being a grown-up. After paying rent on time for a couple months and going to the dentist by yourself, you get the feeling that your life is in order. And then you realize you didn't pay your hot water bill as you stand in a freezing-cold shower trying to get shampoo out of your eyes without becoming a human Popsicle.

Even though adulthood did creep up on me ever so slowly, the one instance I definitively realized I was finally growing up was the time I became a full-blown morning person.

I had spent my post-high school years—and all

non-school days of the first nineteen years of my life—
avoiding the time between six and eleven a.m. You could
reliably find me fast asleep during those hours. Probably because I had stayed up too late on Tumblr, got lost
in the third season of *Gilmore Girls* (again), or binged
on sour candy at three a.m. and went into a sugar coma.
Whatever the reason, there wasn't even a slight chance
I was going to meet you for breakfast. Brunch maybe,
but no early bird special was tempting enough to lose
precious sleep over. I saw people who had active mornings as superhuman. Such willpower! Such self-control!
They would go for runs and eat egg whites with spinach.
They would go to farmers' markets and come home with
reasonably priced jams and fresh-cut daisies wrapped
in brown paper. It was fascinating to me. How did they
operate on such a high-functioning level with barely any
sleep? Did they have a caffeine IV? Were they a special
breed of human that required no rest to operate on a day-
to-day basis?

It was in what can only be described as a moment of extreme genius and mental clarity that I discovered these people simply went to bed at a reasonable hour every night. They had instituted a self-imposed curfew. They hit the hay during double digits. Eleven, ten thirty, maybe even ten if they were really ambitious. Absolute insanity. How was the human body even capable of going to bed that early before you turn fifty? I was baffled. If I called it a night before two a.m., I considered myself the queen of REM. I always had to mindlessly stare at my TV for at least three hours before bed—where did they fit that essential activity into their daily routine? I didn't believe I was physically capable of turning in early. I chalked it up, as many lazy teenagers and prospective adults do, to being a night owl. My biology must be wired for late nights and even later mornings. If I had done even a smidge of research, I would have learned that no one is actually a night owl or an early bird. We're all either lazy or we're down to get a jump on the day. It's not like it takes an insane amount of willpower to go to bed when the moon is still out. Nonetheless I was a self-labeled "night owl." Not a great excuse for my lack of open hours, but I stuck to my timetable and groaned and grumbled whenever I had a morning meeting or anything that couldn't wait until after lunch to deal with.

Then, being a grown-ass, successful woman happened. I finally landed my first real acting gig—after thirty soul-crushing auditions, one stuck. I was costarring in a series that shot in a high school with tall, sunny windows facing inward down the hallways. This prompted the director to want to use natural light in many if not all of our scenes. This meant we had to race against daylight to get all the shots we needed for that workday before it got too dark outside. In film terms, that means your call time to arrive on set is going to be early. I'm talking ass-crack-of-dawn early. I mean my-bedtime-is-my-call-time early. My average arrival time on set was five a.m. I had a couple four fifteen a.m.'s. I typically got off work at eight p.m. That meant if I wanted even a semblance of a good night's rest, I'd have to drive home in a zombielike stupor, take off my caked-on set makeup, scarf down a protein bar or microwavable enchilada, kiss my boyfriend while also brushing my teeth, and then fall into bed. My life had no variance during that month of filming. It was just wake up, work, go home, sleep. Wake up, work, go home, sleep. Wakeupworkgohomesleep—on repeat for twenty days.

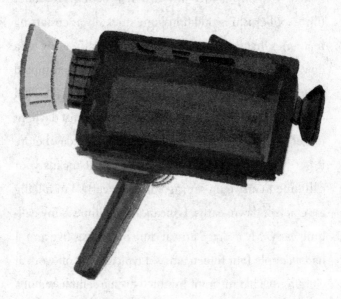

I'm actually grateful for that hellish schedule. It taught me what it's like to work on a job you actually have to get out of bed and put on pants for. Most of my YouTube career has been on my own terms. Which in practice has meant no pants. It also means that if I want to make a video and post it the same day, I do it. This job was a different kind of demanding. I was on someone else's clock. I also had very specific and dedicated time off.

Sometimes I got weekends off during the shoot, a couple days here and there. It taught me how to enjoy the time off I did have. I strived to make every waking hour count. Those were my catch-up-on-life days. I could have more than a three-word conversation with my boyfriend. Our daily interaction would amount to more than, "Good day?" "Yeah." *dives face-first into bed* I could also chat with my friends and assure them that I had not been kidnapped or held against my will. That I was just working insane hours and my eye bags were an indication of fatigue, not struggle against my captor or heroin usage. I could eat real food for more than an hour break between emotional scenes where I threw fits and ripped up papers and completely exhausted myself. Days off meant I didn't have to scarf down a burrito just to get back on set. I could take naps. REAL naps. All day if I wanted to! My time was my own. It was heaven.

Like any sane human, I wanted my days off to last forever. *But* I also didn't want to completely throw off my workday sleeping schedule. What was a grown-ass woman to do? I had been waking up at four thirty every day, and it would be a real shock to the system if I woke up past eight a.m. for two days straight. The delicate balance of sleep that my body had been working under would be completely out of whack! So I kept waking up early. Even on my off days. On Saturdays, I would set my alarm for around six thirty a.m. I stuck to this schedule even if I knew I wasn't shooting for two or more days. I would spend the extra hours getting coffee or sitting in the crisp morning air, listening to the sounds of nature. As my mornings got more and more pretentious— artisanal coffee, differentiating between birdcalls, using my actual stove to cook breakfast rather than going to a drive-through—they got more and more marvelous. Every day, I would force myself to get up early, and it began to feel . . . magical.

Waking up at six a.m. on a Saturday feels sacrilegious at first, but then you get addicted to the solitude. It was like I was the only person left on earth. No one was on the roads. The Starbucks drive-through was blissfully empty.

BREAKFAST BURRITO

FRUIT

SPINACH

The air was dewy and energized with the feeling of possibility. I sat in silence, swaddled in a blanket, sipping my English breakfast tea and reading books I never had time for. I would make breakfast with my boyfriend. Spinach and egg whites. No joke. We would take excursions to the beach and watch the sunrise. We'd make breakfast sandwiches and sit in the sand munching on them while enjoying the fresh air. There was some seriously romantic shit going on early in the morning. I began to look forward to a ten thirty p.m. bedtime so I would be up and at 'em the next day.

Even after my final workday on set, I found myself waking up before seven a.m. The first night when Will wondered why I didn't want to stay up later and finish another episode of *Stranger Things*, I played it off like my body hadn't yet gotten back to its normal rhythm. I was trying to hide the importance that my mornings held in my heart. As the days wore on, I would pretend to nestle into his shoulder during nighttime movies in order to take covert naps and maintain my sleep schedule. For me, for this new grown-up I'd become, the allure of a morning workout followed by a well-rounded breakfast was just too enticing. No Netflix binge was tempting enough to stay up for. All my social engagements became early afternoon affairs.

Then a week of getting up early went by. Spinach was still being consumed. I couldn't keep my eyes open past eleven p.m. My precious morning was like a drug I had to have at the same time every day. I was addicted. Fortunately, for this first little while, Will gave in and played along with my crazy morning shenanigans. He had enjoyed our excursions when our weekends were sacred, when my crazy shooting schedule gave us no time other than the hours we made for each other. Now, he grumbled when I shook his shoulders at six thirty a.m., wide eyed like a crack addict. I pushed him to spring out of bed in the morning, go to the gym for a bit. (Yeah, I got Will Darbyshire to run next to me on a treadmill. I deserve a medal of some kind.)

Not surprisingly, the dam eventually broke. Will had had ENOUGH of all this green juice and morning-walks-into-the-sunrise bullshit. He was a Brit, goddamn it. He loved his sleep. He would sit in bed for days if he could do so without the introduction of bedsores. Who was I to deny him his inalienable human rights? But the problem was, he didn't just want his normal sleep schedule back; he wanted us to return to being night owls *together*.

As a sort of attempt at reentry, he asked me to go to a late showing at the movies. Sugar, excitement, *and* a public place?? How was I going to make my impossibly early bedtime with these kind of late-night shenanigans??? And in that moment, the exact moment I tried to refuse seeing *Finding Dory* at eight thirty p.m., I was shocked to find I was a crusty, old, no-fun adult. Will was right. I was disgusted by what a twisted, boring version of myself I was morphing into. What was the next irritatingly adult thing I was going to get into? Five a.m. cycling classes? Wheatgrass shots? Acai bowls for breakfast, lunch, and dinner? No. I was going to cling to my fading youth! I was going to be spontaneous, rage against my elderly internal clock, be a kid again! I couldn't believe how quickly I had succumbed to adulthood. It was such a slippery slope.

When we arrived at the movie theater, I beelined for the concessions stand. It was GROSS how much I was prepared to consume in the next hour and a half. I got a tub of flossy pink cotton candy, a large popcorn that I drizzled with an obscene amount of butter (that shit is definitely not actually a dairy product of any kind), AND a large Coke. Not even Diet Coke, regular Coke. FULL-SUGAR COKE. I was going on a rampage. I don't even like soda. We headed to theater seven, found our seats, and situated our worrying amount of snacks (Will also got malted milk balls and Sour Patch Kids).

I was trying so hard to keep up my hard-core mentality. Who knew cinema could become an X sport? I was shifting in my seat constantly, attempting to keep myself uncomfortable, because I knew if I found a spot in my chair that hugged my butt just right and made me feel warm and cuddled, I'd be a goner. Will offered his shoulder in an attempt at a snuggle, but I refused politely. I had my eye on the prize. I was going to make it through the movie. I was going to enjoy the CRAP out of this. As the trailers rolled and the lights dimmed, I held on to every vestige of willpower that I contained.

I fell asleep within fifteen minutes. I was OUT.

I spent the entire movie getting woken up by Will as I attempted to use him as a pillow. He was surprisingly less likely to give me cuddles when he realized I was lying on him with the sleepy force of a drowsy manatee. But I persevered. I didn't tap out and leave. Still, on the drive home, I felt like I had merely seen a preview of a film I'd actually seen the entirety of. There were some fish? And they couldn't remember where they were or who their parents were? I felt an odd connection to the character of Dory that night. I was in a haze and all I wanted to do was sleep. I played Diplo to keep me pumped and to remind me that there were people my age raging and doing drugs and being general crazy people without blinking an irresponsible eye, while I was struggling with participating in a movie date night that literally required nothing physically but to stay awake. I was a sad case.

The next morning at seven a.m., I woke up with a start. My alarm hadn't gone off. In fact, I hadn't set an alarm so I could make an attempt at sleeping in. But my body had different plans. I stared at the ceiling and tried to keep my mind from realizing it was go time. I had to poop, man. I needed my morning tea. I couldn't lie in with my boyfriend and cuddle because my brain was demanding I start my day. I was living under a dictatorship ruled by my circadian rhythm. I was done with this nonsense. I couldn't do it anymore. I'd have to sacrifice my precious mornings. I legitimately wasn't seeing as much of Will as I used to. I wasn't up bonding with him by bingeing some terrible but amazing cartoon we heard about on Reddit. I wasn't giggling with him over Netflix series or cuddles or Oreos or ANYTHING.

That following weekend, I took a stand. I would stay in bed and not leave until noon. It might have been a bit excessive, but this was all-out internal warfare, and I had a new strategy. I was going to force my body to reverse itself just like I'd forced it to change in the first place. So I made it to midnight Friday night with a careful combination of small doses of caffeine throughout the day (I think I drank a good five cups of tea) and a large amount of entertaining television. I'm pretty sure we watched an entire season of *Friends*. I was determined to break my cycle. I had my entire life to be productive and active in the morning. I'd save my thirties for that!

Screw being an actual human until you absolutely have to. I made the choice to be a lazy piece of crap in the morning again. But I did it for the right reasons: I examined my priorities and made a conscious decision to do what would allow me to enjoy my life to the fullest right now.

There's nothing that designates you as a correct adult. People talk about adulthood like it requires fitting into a socially agreed-upon standard of living. But that doesn't really determine adulthood. Being an adult just means making educated decisions for yourself that you think will make your life better and your own. The responsibility of adulthood is pretty inevitable. But you can adult however you want. If that means early mornings and egg-white omelets are your favorite routine, that's totally fine. My routine just happens to be a large amount of laziness in the a.m. If that's what makes me joyful in my life, then I'm adulting correctly. I'd rather be tired and grumpy at a café for an eight a.m. meeting than miss out on the time I spend goofing around with Will doing something stupid like making gluten-free brownies at one a.m. and then watching him slice his hand open trying to take the label off a new wooden spoon. Even if we end up at the ER. Actually, I could live without that specific incident, but it's those kinds of adventures I know I'll remember and look back on semi-fondly later on in life.

You, too, need to find your life comfort zone and pursue what makes you categorize a day as a "good day." Relentlessly search for your good day, and don't let someone else's ideal affect your own! Some may see my night-owl-ness as lazy and sluggish. I see it as an opportunity to be closer to my boyfriend and enjoy nighttime in a city as interesting as LA. You can't let weird rules or codes of conduct in life dictate how you behave. Who wrote those codes? Who told you that you should only eat kale and raw almonds your whole life? Someone who is just as human and mistake-prone as you are. And probably deficient in several essential vitamins. I'm not saying that you should question someone far more educated than you on a specific matter. I'm not going to scoff at my gynecologist if she thinks I need to take care of my yeast infection. However, you should live your life with a hint of curiosity behind every choice you make. Why do you feel it necessary to buy a stand-alone mixer for your kitchen? Is it because you've been wanting one for months and can't wait to get to baking? Or because you want to LOOK like you might start baking at some point? Stop getting stuff you don't need because you feel like every proper adult should have it.

Whether you're a morning person, or someone like me who can barely stand how comfortable her bed is, you're doing all right. I promise. It's okay to make choices that might conflict with the lifestyles of others. In fact, I encourage it. Never let the dissonant voice of another person throw off your groove if you know you're making the right decisions for yourself. Just make sure you're always questioning your own rituals and the daily rituals of others. Let that spark of excitement over trying something new rule your day every now and then. Never settle into something only to realize you hate doing it in the first place. Habits are hard to break, and once you've gotten into one, only you can regain enough control to get yourself out of it. Own your life. As cliché as it sounds, you only get one shot at a great one.

You're independent now; it's up to you to determine

how you want your days to go by. It's a heavy responsibility, but you know how you like your life. Personally, I take
mine sunny-side up. But only after eleven a.m. And with
a side of hot sauce.

AN ODE TO MY BUTT

Little-known secret: I have a juicy tush. Maybe it's more peachy than juicy, but my ass is large and in charge. People don't believe me until they behold the jiggle with their own eyes. You might get a glimpse of it on a night out with me. As I make a (poor) attempt at dropping it low, you'd detect a slight wobble in my derriere. Just a small hint of the wondrous, rotund secrets my bandage dress has cloistered away. Like a blind and neutered snake, my butt dips and sways with little care toward either coordination or sex appeal. But it's still there, hanging off the end of me. And I'm well aware of it. Especially while jeans shopping.

I wasn't always sitting jaded in my ill-fitting jeans. I only got the first warning jiggle of a budding butt at seventeen. And at the tender age of thirteen, I once attempted to stuff my underwear. Unfortunately, I was not the sophisticated sort, and I discovered silicone butt pads way past my time of need. So I did what any insecure, ass-less girl does when faced with a body-augmenting challenge: I grabbed a roll of toilet paper and got to work. I folded and molded and sculpted until I had what I imagined underwear models gazed upon each and every morning in the mirror. While eating breakfast with my family, I wore a long cardigan to hide my handiwork. In the car ride to school, I hovered ever so slightly above the seat to ensure my masterpiece survived the journey.

By the time second period rolled around, I had already excused myself to the bathroom a solid five times to make sure nothing had shifted or flattened during class. My lackluster thigh and ass muscles were burning from my self-inflicted perma-hover. If anything, I gained a good pound of strength from basically doing the insecure middle schooler's version of a Brazilian butt workout. As predicted, any ounce of enjoyment or self-esteem I got out of my new and improved backside was completely overshadowed by the inconvenience of it all. That wasn't me. I was too lazy to be that bootylicious all the time. Being a try-hard was exhausting and gave me very little pleasure. No one even noticed or admired my effort!

Eventually, I got the butt my thirteen-year-old self had slightly worrying dreams about. And yet, as puberty set in for me and certain body parts received the advantage of accelerated growth, I realized my new bodily proportions were just slightly askew. My butt jumped ahead of the pack while my scrawny legs were thrust into the difficult job of supporting it. Sometimes I look in the mirror and picture my lower half as a grape with two toothpicks jutting out of it. Boobs? Prepubescent. Ass? Enough for two. Now, normally I'm happy with my caboose, but recently

I've had to open up an uncomfortable dialogue with the poor thing. It won't let me find the right size for any of my clothes. A dress that fits my itty-bitty titties and my balloon butt? Not happening. Ordering pants online going just off my waist size? Prepare to split a side seam. For once I'd love to put on bottoms other than sweatpants that fit my ass, thighs, and waist correctly and flatteringly. Is that so much to ask for? C'mon, puberty fairy godmother, step out of retirement and give me some childbearing hips to match! At least then I could justify tailoring everything I buy for the rest of my life.

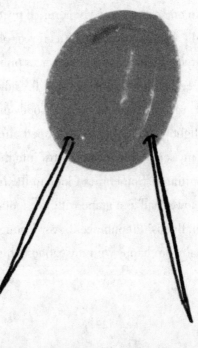

So was I satisfied and happy once I had a butt, in exchange for an endless war against traditional clothing sizing? No. Inevitably I found something new about my body to dislike and obsess over. It's not like I actually have something drastically wrong with my body at any given time, I just choose to make myself feel bad for things I can't control. Like my skin, or my butt. I won't say I'm particularly struggling with my body image at the moment, but the past couple months my acne has come out to play. And let me tell you, it is easy to boil my entire personhood down into each of those embarrassing marks on my face. Hey, it's me! The girl constantly battling against adult acne! What a fun thing to deal with in your twenties!

I spent a solid ten months last year fighting round after round of angry abusive acne on my face. I thought it was my birth control. Then I chalked it up to dairy in my diet. Then I obsessively washed my pillowcases, thinking it was my oily night face causing all this ruckus. In the end, making a dermatology appointment changed my life. If you have the funds or decent health insurance, get a professional to check out your skin. I wish I had found an acne routine that worked for me sooner! I can't tell you how much more confident and unabashed I feel when I walk out the door with no makeup on my face. Such a liberating feeling! I don't have to hide behind a cake face to feel comfortable enough to show my skin anymore. For those of you really struggling with acne, just know it's not your fault and you will find a solution to it. Pimples super-duper suck, and I wouldn't wish them on my worst enemy.

I will never be perfectly happy with my physical appearance. I've accepted that. But I'm going to let you in on a little secret. NO ONE IS. I live in LA and I've overheard five-foot-ten rail-thin models complain about love handles in the middle of ordering kale salads with "dressing on the side, please and thank you."

No matter how much you critique and fix yourself, you will always find a new physical problem in need of fixing. It's taken me awhile to realize this, but every time I see someone and think, "Damn, she's gorgeous," it's always when the person in question is not giving a single fuck about their appearance. Sure, red-carpet glam teams exist for a reason, but if you want to see true beauty, do a quick search on Google of, "Cara Delevingne hungover eating cheeseburger." That girl looks like she has lost the capacity to give a fuck. Obviously, she's a supermodel with genetically perfect facial features, but I admire someone with such an overwhelming amount of pressure to appear beautiful and the simultaneous will to look immaculately human while going ham on a greasy bag of McDonald's.

My body idols are not the same as they were when I was a teenager. I was used to seeing tiny girls with skinny arms gracing every cover of *Vogue*, and I thought that was a standard I needed to hold myself to. Now I realize how important that person is internally behind their physical appearance. There's no point in being a "perfect" body type if you're a nasty little fart on the inside. Not that I think there is such a thing as a "perfect" body type. I no longer strive to look like fitspo girls on Tumblr. I don't need to put that pressure on myself. First of all, it's completely unrealistic. I'm not going to lie to you and say, "Nobody looks like that! She's too thin!" Because, yeah, some people looking just like that actually do exist in the real world.

What is unrealistic is expecting your randomly

predetermined genes and body type to fit a societal standard that is not meant to make you feel included. A single "perfect" body type is elitist. Everyone should be able to have their perfect body. By setting a physical standard based on one particular form, you disqualify entire gene pools, races, and cultures from feeling celebrated. It's not fair that for centuries the 1 percent got to determine what defines beauty. Thanks to the internet, we finally live in a time where anyone can set the bar for attractiveness. Now everyone has an opportunity to feel appreciated and celebrated. You can go online and see women of all shapes and sizes who look gorgeous. You can find someone who looks eerily similar to you and is rocking the shit out of a crop top you felt too self-conscious to buy. It's empowering and comforting in a way. The body positivity I've seen on Twitter, Tumblr, and Instagram makes me proud to be an internet personality. I think a flawless body is whatever body makes you feel most comfortable. It's up to you whether that means working out every day and eating kale, or doing absolutely zero but enjoying the body nature gave you. Neither one is a bad thing inherently as long as you're happy. And ultimately, that's all that

matters.

One crazy thing that makes me feel a little bit better is the fact that bodies go in and out of style just like clothes. If you're super thin and twiggy, you were the height of popularity in the nineties. If you are athletic and muscular, the eighties were your time to shine. Nowadays we seem to love thick hips and big boobies. Whatever your figure might be, you are a fashion icon spanning across decades! You just might be ahead of your time. Or a relic of a different era. Everyone is going to be smitten all over again when you come back into style.

Not that it actually matters what opinions anyone else has over your body. People might tell you that you're too thin. Others might say you're too chubby. You will never be able to win until you are self-assured enough to give a big ol' middle finger to everyone all around. Fitting a cookie-cutter ideal of beauty is ridiculous and stupid. Even if it was theoretically possible, I wouldn't want to have a perfect body. I want my straight hips and jiggly ass and baby face. I want all the weird moles on my skin and crooked teeth and big pores that define me as an independent human. No one in the history of mankind has ever been exactly identical to me. That is an incredible and humbling idea. I am the only me that will ever exist, and regardless of how insecure I can feel at times, I'm going to do a damn good job at me-ing!

Padding my butt was a landmark event in my life. It marked the last time I gave a real fuck about what other people thought about my body. I might still get a little offended if someone calls me a chubbier Amanda Bynes, but I'm pretty used to that by now. I'm just happy to say that I am going through my twenties enjoying myself and my body without giving it the same extreme regimen I thought necessary in my teens. Go easy on yourself and your body. You only get one of these flesh bags to keep you going in life, and you should give it a break. It's gotten you this far! Take a minute to find some things that you really love about yourself, and give them a good old-fashioned compliment. Look at my calf muscles popping out—I love you, athletic little things! They say your eyes are the window to the soul—well then, my eyebrows must be the tasteful drapes bringing the whole vision together; their hairy structured beauty is beyond compare. We didn't forget about you, eyes! Look at how nice and green you are. Statistically, you are considered the most attractive eye color by society. So you have that going for you! Even if I can't see shit out of you. 20/20 vision my (unstuffed) ass.

LET'S TALK ABOUT SEX UNTIL I MAKE YOU MILDLY TO EXTREMELY UNCOMFORTABLE

You're allowed to enjoy sex. Like, you're allowed to really, really like sex. Outside of marriage. With someone who might not be your "one true love." As someone who was raised in a religious household, I never knew this could be true. I don't think I've actually ever heard my mom use the word "sex" in a positive way. I grew up on the internet, so I sort of knew that being sex-negative in our modern world was crap. Statistics back it up: per several Advocates for You reviews of federally funded evaluations, if you really want teenagers to get pregnant and raise babies in unstable households, teach them abstinence-only sex education. I guess that's why liberal-minded schools are always hurling condoms in every direction. At fourteen years old, I hadn't had a single conversation with an adult close to me about anything sex-related. Until I got to high school I was legitimately worried about the fact that men apparently peed inside you to get you pregnant. I thought the whole act of sexual intercourse must be one of the grossest parts of humanity.

I remember in eighth grade, a month before school was let out for the summer holiday, an announcement went out schoolwide that we would be participating in ABC classes the following week. All of the immature, sexually stunted kids in my grade got so excited. ABC stood for Abstinence by Choice. Which should really be abbreviated as ABYPPOGHC (Abstinence by Your Parents', Pastor's, or God Himself's Choice). This "class" was a one-day seminar that would supposedly teach us about sex. Most kids were just excited that we would be let out of school at noon after the presentation was over. That Monday, sweaty with the anticipation of some sexual gratification, all two hundred fourteen-year-olds were separated by gender and led into private rooms. Boys and girls obviously couldn't be taught the same integral knowledge of sex together lest they become ashamed of their gender or sexuality. *eye rolls to infinity*

There I am sitting in this dark room with eighty other girls, and I'm just praying that they'll explain the whole "peeing inside you to get pregnant" thing. A woman enters the room, wheeling in a portable projector. She has this terrifying, stony look on her face. She explains that she has come to our school to warn us of the unholy nature of sex. She wants us to be fully aware of the consequences of entertaining any carnal delights. As she slides her hand through a greasy mop of curly gray hair, she flicks a switch and the projector sputters to life. Apparently the slides she wanted to show us were so ancient, they were the type of preloaded stills that had to be clicked into place to be seen. One of the slides was already coming to life on the screen as the machine whirred and attempted to warn us of what was to come. It appeared to be a lumpy piece of roast beef with some mold emanating from the depths of its folds. I think you know where this is going.

"This is what your genitals will look like if you have sex out of marriage and contract chlamydia," she said, bored stiff while clicking to the next slide. This was not her first lackluster, sexually educational rodeo. A picture of a severely wounded baby bird cloistered away in a twiggy, hairy-looking nest popped up next. "This is what your partner's genitals will look like if you have sex out of marriage and he contracts chlamydia." She went on like this as the slides became more and more grotesque, each one clicking into place in my brain with severity. Gonorrhea did not look fun. Syphilis DEFINITELY did not look fun. After she had finished strong with a story of how rampant and destructive herpes could be, our "sex ed" teacher was done. She shut off the projector as each one of the children she'd just scarred for life silently begged someone to get rid of their sex organs. I didn't want a vagina if it could cause me so much trouble. Before we all recovered from the series of bombshells, she passed out little pieces of paper that looked like business cards. Each card had the same manifesto printed on it:

> *I will not act upon impure thoughts or have any sexual relations before I'm married, with Jesus Christ as my witness.*

We were then all given pens that said ABC down the sides of them and told to sign the back of the cards. As if we were entering into a legal relationship with Jesus. He was going to make SURE we weren't getting any behind the bleachers after football games. I signed the card and looked around as everyone else did the same. We had no idea how weird a concept signing a virginity pact was. We were fourteen and we were being told that we shouldn't explore a huge facet of our humanity. And since we had all been raised with this same philosophy, all of us agreed. I kept that card in my wallet for a little while.

Finally, all the guys we'd been segregated from rejoined us, and both sides avoided eye contact. They had obviously been shown the same slides.

For some reason, that card burned a hole in my wallet when I got into high school. I felt a guilty weight every time I spotted the card while trying to reach for my Tropical Smoothie loyalty card. I couldn't take it anymore and decided I needed a symbolic place to lay my virgin-

ity to rest. So I dumped the card with my scribbly signature on it right in the trash. I wish I had saved it. I would frame it and put it on prominent display somewhere in my apartment.

I look back now on

what my sex education entailed, and it makes me sad. I didn't learn anything about my own body or how beautiful it can be. I didn't know what my vagina was. I didn't know that the clitoris existed. No one thought those things were worth mentioning. We didn't even talk about periods even though several girls in my grade were already struggling with theirs. School didn't broach the topic of safe sex. In our educators' eyes, the safest form of intercourse was not having it in the first place. I had no idea what a penis actually looked like past all the herpes and sores. I was taught to be scared of my body and my partner's body. We were warned about all the bad—never told to celebrate the good—things that could come of our genitals.

I hope that one day even conservative communities can understand the importance of educating young teens about their sexuality. You don't have to be a sex-negative religious person. You can still abstain from sex and understand its importance at the same time. It's a primal human urge. It's older and more ingrained in us than our sentience. Better to be aware and understanding than ignorant and left in a dangerous situation.

***

In the end, it was porn that taught me more about sex than my private school or my parents ever did. The first porn I ever watched was *One Night in Paris*. Yes, Paris Hilton. The video embarrassingly revolved around blow jobs, but I still gained some valuable carnal wisdom within those twenty minutes of male-centric pleasure. I didn't understand why you would willingly let a dude pee in your mouth. By the end of the video I was confused. Disgusted. But mostly fascinated. I went down a sordid rabbit hole that night. I learned what BBW meant (Big Beautiful Woman). I learned what being uncircumcised actually meant. (I still think it looks like the penis is chilly and has to wear a turtleneck. It's kinda cute, in a gross, penis-y way.) I was thoroughly interested in all the unfiltered smut my greedy little pubescent eyes beheld. My masturbation habits got . . . upsetting. Like, I got visibly excited when the seventh-period bell rang to indicate school was over—so I could run home and rub one out. I know you're probably making a really grossed-out face right now reading this. You're thinking to yourself, "Jesus Christ, give it a rest, you tiny nympho." But I want to be honest about my experience with my sexuality. Most women feel pressure to keep their sex lives to themselves.

And that leads to a lack of education and the stigma that women don't enjoy sex or can't derive pleasure from sex. It's beyond ridiculous.

I didn't tell anyone about my habits. I knew guys at my school were watching porn and masturbating but I hadn't heard of any girls doing it. The guys were never ashamed to talk about their habits, while the girls wouldn't dare bring it up. That was too taboo, and impure, and downright unladylike. So I kept it to myself. To be honest, I still think the most hard-core Christians were probably the smuttiest on the down-low. But my school, also very Christian, was against sex in any capacity other than married, and missionary, and only to make babies. It was socially celebrated to abstain from whacking your weeds. So I just kept it as my special dirty secret.

And then it wasn't until my first real boyfriend that I jumped into that mysterious pool of human anatomy called sexual intercourse. My first time went a little something like this: I turned to my boyfriend and told him I wanted to have sex. We had fooled around, and had done basically, as they say, "everything but sex." Granted, all sexual acts are sex. They just might be outercourse rather than intercourse. Only having given a blow job does not mean you haven't had sex. You've had oral sex. It's not like any kind of roundabout way of getting sexy with someone else "doesn't count." (I always find it hilarious in movies when the gossipy girls are having a sleepover and talking about the supposedly slutty girl at the school by saying she's "done everything but." Such a weird trope that we're all going to look back on and find bizarre in ten years.) But back to the story. I was impatient and didn't care about following the rules of conduct that my family had put in place. I had watched plenty of porn and read a mountain of articles on safe sex like the horny but cautious teenager that I was. I asked my boyfriend to drive us to get condoms.

We went to the local CVS, and under the seemingly blaring fluorescent lights, I browsed the sexual health section like I was about to steal something. I must have looked so sketchy, but I was just trying to avoid anyone from my hometown seeing me buying contraceptives. God forbid Mrs. Nancy from down the street notice my sinful lifestyle. My parents would get me GOOD if they knew what lusty atrocities were occurring after they went to bed. I slipped a pack of heavily lubed condoms up my hoodie sleeve, like I was smuggling drugs, and headed to the cash register. I paid for them, ran to the car, and spent the ride back to my boyfriend's parents' house staring at the weird latex circles that were going to prevent me from having babies at seventeen. It was an odd moment. I had been the catalyst for this whole situation. My boyfriend was silent. I could tell he was nervous. I'm pretty sure I intimidated the crap out of him. No girls (that I knew of) in my hometown were this forthright with what they wanted sexually, but damn it, I was curious.

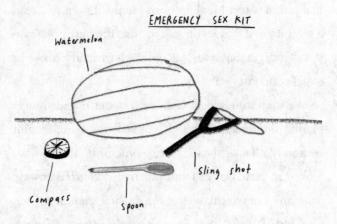

EMERGENCY SEX KIT

Watermelon

sling shot

Compass

Spoon

The actual act of losing my virginity made me realize how silly the idea of virginity is in the first place. There is nothing "precious" or "special" about fumbling around with a condom for twenty minutes while cursing under your breath. Neither of us orgasmed that night, which was to be expected. After everything had been performed, I lay down next to my boyfriend and thought about how anticlimactic the whole thing was. I also registered the fact that I didn't feel a shred of guilt. I had been led to believe that Satan himself would come to claim your soul if you had sex before marriage, but nothing bad happened. I didn't get a disease. I didn't even orgasm. Why had people been hyping this up for so long? I honestly thought about proposing a second round just because I didn't think we'd done it right. Sparks weren't shooting out of my vagina. That would probably be a terrifying fire hazard if it actually happened, but it just didn't add up to me. Why was sex such a coveted thing if it ended up being so . . . lackluster?

By the way, I've got some theories about the whole concept of women having a "carnal treasure" or being "precious flowers" that need special tending. Vaginas are seriously resilient, guys, they can withstand a lot. We GIVE ACTUAL BIRTH TO REAL HUMANS through our ladybits. Do you know how wide a baby's head is? Our vaginas are miraculous stretchy marvels. Women are metal. And vaginas *don't* stretch out after you have sex. Your vagina widens when you're properly aroused, but even after giving birth, the vagina goes back to relatively the same diameter. When you have sex, you're not being dirtied, or soiled, or ruined. The idea of "popping your cherry" is just excess hymen—skin flaps just inside your vagina—being ripped. I popped my cherry when I started masturbating. Your hymen isn't a large ribbon outside a new sports center in town waiting to be cut so everyone can barge in after the chop. And similarly, being sexually active doesn't mean you're automatically open for business all around town.

So how does one actually have enjoyable intercourse? I think the golden trio is enthusiasm, willingness to learn, and practice. I hardly think your partner will *begrudgingly* comply with a couple extra sessions here and there to try something new. Sex is the most fun activity you can do with your clothes off! Other than naked watersliding. (It makes you feel like a seal.) For me to have enjoyable sex, I had to learn my body first. You can't expect someone to know how to please you when you don't know how to please yourself. Like I discussed earlier, I loved masturbating. I had it down to a science. But if you only orgasm in one way, it can become the ONLY way you orgasm. And that's no fun. Switch up your positions. Learn how to orgasm in different ways.

Learn how to enjoy the act of giving oral sex. And just as important, learn how to let yourself enjoy receiving oral. I know that sounds like a given, but before Will, I was way too self-conscious to let someone party downtown. I'm not saying you have to get down with every sexual act, but it's good to be open to expanding your horizons as long as you're comfortable. I definitely learned what I liked in bed through experience. I went from not knowing what circumcision was to owning my sexuality and really learning how to enjoy the journey of sexual discovery. Sure, there was a lot of fumbling around with condoms, and not getting it in right away, but ultimately, it all led to a healthy relationship with sex that I'll be able to enjoy for years to cum—I mean come.

Learn to ask for what you want, and stay away from people who make you feel bad for it! This is a controversial opinion, but I sometimes advocate watching porn with your partner. You can find strong feminist porn that isn't degrading to women; there are tons of sites online that are made by women, for women. Take advantage of them as much as you can, so we can support a female-positive sex industry. Plus, they tend to have ladies actually coming in them, not just faking it. Watching porn can help you realize new possibilities for yourself.

I just remembered that I also need to emphasize to you lovely people that orgasm alone does not always indicate that the sex was good. You can have amazing sex and not come. Don't let that pressure ruin your time! Sex is more than reaching orgasm. Sex is a bonding of two bodies and minds. It's release. It's supposed to be fun. I always felt like my ex would get incredibly annoyed if I couldn't come. It got to the point where I'd fake it just so I didn't have to deal with him pouting for the next hour. It made me more nervous and more anxious every time we wanted to have sex. Granted, I was also too self-conscious to allow him to go down on me, but it

got to the point where I never came again in our relationship, because I just wanted to fake it and move on. This went on for two years. TWO YEARS. I've learned my lesson since then. To quote one of the greatest minds of our time, Ms. Nicki Minaj: "I demand that I climax. I think women should demand that." Not that you necessarily have to come every time you have sex, but if you want to, you should have a partner who wants to help you get there.

Sex is a partnership. Even if it's only for a night. You are coming together to achieve a common goal, and if one member of that team is slacking, the entire operation is compromised. Learn what you like in bed, and don't settle for less. I spent so long faking orgasms so that I could make someone else happy. I would just go along with another person's pleasure while not facilitating my own. I only realized how silly it was when I met someone who I felt more comfortable with, someone I could talk to about positions I liked or techniques that worked on my body, and who was just as forthright as I was with his wants and desires. Get what you want, as long as it is wanted by both parties. Just don't be discouraged if it takes you some time to reach orgasm. And, for the sake of other women who might have sex with your current partner in the future, don't fake it. It teaches men the wrong things to do in bed. Unless there's something disastrously wrong that could be corrected with a simple conversation, it doesn't have to be a huge deal if you can't come, and your partner should know that.

Being a sexual woman doesn't mean you're a slut. It means you own your body, and you'll do with it what you please. On the flip slide, you also don't have to have sex! Being careful about who you have sex with—or not wanting to have sex—doesn't make you a prude. You're allowed to feel however you want to about your own body, and NO ONE can dictate what you do with it except for yourself. Above all, don't let anyone else pressure you or make you feel uncomfortable in a sexual situation. You don't deserve that, and you don't need to put up with it. You don't owe anyone sex just because you've chosen to have sex before, or because they want it. And if anything happens to you without your consent, please tell someone. Don't let sexual assault go because you're worried about your image. You have nothing to be ashamed about, and women who come forward about their assaults are actively helping destigmatize and end the crisis of rape and assault. At the same time, if you don't want to talk about it, don't. Rape and sexual assault are personal attacks, and you get to handle them however you feel ready to.

We need to stop perpetuating the idea that women can't or shouldn't be active sexual people of our own free will. We need to stop teaching young girls that they should feel guilty about having sex. We need to *start* teaching young girls how to listen to their own bodies and how to have safe, consensual sex. So don't listen to anyone who makes you feel ashamed for your sexual choices. Don't let that stupid frat guy in your class belittle you for not sleeping with him, or for sleeping with his best friend. He just wishes he was getting some. You do you, and let others do themselves. Also, don't ever refer to another girl as a slut. It only makes you look like you don't respect women's authority over their bodies enough to allow another woman to enjoy hers. Be secure in what you've got going on. Be that friend who high-fives her girlfriends when they get some, and always have condoms ready for that girl in your dorm who never has safe sex. Be the cool mom.

But don't actually become a mom until you're ready for that commitment. Research contraceptive options until you feel comfortable with one. I've been through nearly every contraceptive option you can throw up a vagina or take in a pill form. I've taken two different versions of hormone-based contraceptive pills. I've used condoms. Spermicide. I have a special place in my heart for the sponge, even though, when I used it, I would get intense yeast infections. (Plus, they were really annoying to put in every time I wanted to get down and dirty. You inserted them right before sex, and there's nothing quite as libido destroying as putting a foamy, chemical-smelling plug up your vagina.) Elaine Benes from *Seinfeld* had the same love-hate relationship with her weird disk of foam that you shove up your womanhood. Elaine has a terrifying moment of fear when she finds out her contraceptive of choice is being discontinued. She doesn't know how she'll be able to have sex once it's gone. That feeling of abandonment is REAL when you fall in love with a birth control and it vanishes. It's extremely difficult to find a contraceptive that works for you without making you miserable in some way. Once you get that perfect match, it's not unlike finding your soul mate. When I was on birth-control pills, I was angry. Like, FURIOUS, 95 percent of the time. I acted like you had murdered my mother when you tried to eat my food out of the fridge.

Don't even consider touching my Flamin' Hot Cheetos. You will lose a hand. And I will relish taking it from your dumb ass.

So someone please get on the whole male birth-control thing! If men had uteruses, we would never have these kind of issues with enormous side effects that we're just supposed to "deal with." It's silly and sexist that women alone are expected to handle the job of preventing pregnancies. For the time being, though, look out for your own sexual health until the medical world can find a preventive medicine that doesn't make men worried their balls are on the line.

If you haven't found your perfect contraceptive yet, take your time. It's a long process to discover what your body vibes with when it comes to sexual health. Go to a gynecologist and have a frank discussion about what you want in a birth control. Talk about your mental health and the general health of your lady parts. Be honest. I went through a period of insane UTIs and yeast infections when Will and I first started dating. After having a little talk with my vagina doctor, she decreed that I was having too much sex, and condoms were irritating my vaginal wall. I relished the first half of her diagnosis, but my delight in being a sex panther only lasted until my burning bladder reminded me what terrible consequences my new love had wrought upon my anatomy.

I've come a long way from the CVS aisle in taking charge of my own sexual health! It's always a balance; what matters is finding the balance that's right for you. I'm using NuvaRing right now, and I'm fairly happy with it. My skin, on the other hand, hates my birth control. I don't think my chin will ever recover from the amount of acne that's sprung up from this cursed thing. But I don't get emotional or angsty or super depressed on Nuva-Ring. I've never been a suicidal person, but some birth controls are scary manipulative. It's crazy how detrimental hormones can be to your mental health. If I didn't hate the feeling of condoms more than life itself, I'd be off birth control faster than you can say, "Estrogen-induced depression." And the only reason I can rely on birth control alone in my sexual relationship is because both my partner and I have been tested and we're monogamous. If you're planning on having sex with multiple partners, always use a barrier method like a condom to prevent STDs, STIs, and all those other scary consequences of unprotected sex. Stay safe, kids.

I'll wrap up this chapter by leaving you with the most important lesson I've learned about sex: Sex isn't scary, and you shouldn't treat it like it is. It can be fun and exciting, but it should never make you feel anxious. You don't have to have sex. You don't have to abstain from sex. You are in control of your own body, and you're allowed to do whatever you want with it. As long as you're not one of those people shoving glass jars up their asses on camera, because that shit is dangerous. Take ownership over your body, and never let someone treat you like you are an object. Because you're not a piece of furniture. You're a human being with a mind, and a soul, and body that is singularly yours to take care of and to take pleasure in. Own that shit. And enjoy all that crazy kinky sex you're hopefully going to have as soon as you're done reading this chapter. I wish you luck—and don't forget to use a condom.

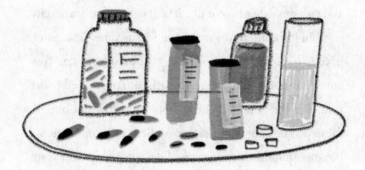

DAD'S NOT FEELING GREAT, GUYS

It's not always a wonderful thing to be an optimist. I learned from a tender young age that it's not necessarily helpful to be overly positive when it comes to the looming presence of a bad outcome. I remember going to school in a naive state of positivity and hopefulness after my dad told me he had prostate cancer. Someone else reacting to that news might feel fear or a sense of duty to be there for her ailing family. But I was only about thirteen when he told me about his illness, so I had the youthful ignorance of someone who thinks nothing can go awry in her life. Looking back, I should have been far more worried.

There was no possible end result in my head other than my dad getting better and never again showing signs of sickness. The cancer wasn't expected to spread, but the doctors also didn't want it to set up camp anytime soon. It needed to be evacuated promptly. Surgeries were scheduled and calendars were marked ominously in red. There's a pretty good success rate when it comes to ridding the body of prostate cancer, and my dad was going to have some very capable robot arms operate on his tumor. My mom bought Tempur-Pedic pillows in a preparatory attempt to curtail my dad's inevitable discomfort post-operation. Meanwhile, my dad figured out how many days he'd be out of work. It was quite a few days.

It didn't really hit me that there could be a chance of disaster until the day of the surgery. As a kid I was exceptionally skilled at compartmentalizing my life woes. I could take in terrible news and turn it into a crossed-fingers prayer that would be answered miraculously. The day my dad went in for surgery, he was meant to come out at roughly the same time he arrived home from work every day. Afterward, I don't recall exactly how he made it from the car to the front door to his bedroom, but I can't imagine it was a good look. When I first ran to cuddle up next to him in bed, he winced, and it really hit me: he was in true and horrible pain. My dad, Mr. Omnipotent and Unflinching, was not feeling great. He had a catheter, which was a bitch to deal with and definitely didn't make for a pain-free recovery. He also had several purple scars etched across his abdomen. He couldn't get out of bed for a while, and they put him on heavy pain medications to help him sleep.

Seeing him this way drastically changed my view on the human condition. Someone I had seen as an anchor of unflappability was suddenly weak and defenseless. For a lot of kids, their dads are their rocks. Someone who can't be hurt. And, now, this person I'd forever seen as impenetrable was suffering from a condition I'd only heard about in a very life-threatening context. I almost didn't believe cancer existed before he had it. It was like a scary unicorn in my mind. Something other people suffered with, but not my close family. Never my parents. Now I could see my own dad dying from this. Death was an even scarier unicorn with a supersharp horn. I had willfully ignored the idea that I could lose someone on this earth before I was fifty. I realized how vulnerable we all are. He kept up the facade of strength, but I could see how tired he got after even just chatting with me for too long. You never want to be in a position where your hero seems human.

I feel strongly connected to my dad. I'd chirped his ear off for most of my childhood while he'd sit and listen to whatever subject I was feeling passionate about. After a long day of work dealing with people far less kind than himself (he owned rental properties and constantly dealt with irritable tenants and contractors trying to squeeze money out of him), he would arrive home tired and ready for an immediate leap into bed. I'd often be waiting up for him so I could shove a book into his hands. He would stay up the extra hour just to read the Redwall series to me. After two chapters of animal impressions and medieval mice adventures, his voice would take on this mumbling butteriness and I'd have to snuggle up under his arm to hear him clearly. I spent most of my childhood attempting to fall asleep while my dad read to me so he would carry me in his arms to bed. I was such a selfish, lazy fuck. I think he enjoyed our mandatory bonding sessions, though. He would pretend to resist when I would bat my eyes up at him and beg to be read to, but he was a softie and gave in every time.

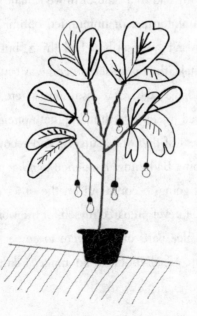

My dad was a very fit and springy guy in his youth. Always down for an adventure. Always down for a day outside in the backyard. He kept up that spirit of athleticism until his prostate surgery. After that, I saw a distinct turning point in his life. He looked a little less bright in the morning. He gained some weight since he was on bed rest, and he spent most of his time reading to himself or out loud to me and my sister. Someone had to help him to the bathroom, and he was always sleeping. He just felt so finite and vulnerable in those weeks.

Seeing my dad in a state of unwell made me realize how silly uninformed or unfounded optimism can be. Optimism isn't necessarily a bad thing, but it can be when you take the optimistic outcome as truth. Be optimistic, but have a dash of realism somewhere in the mix. I had tricked myself into thinking that none of that grueling process of discovery, surgery, and recovery would ever transpire. Bad things happened to *other* people. *My* family was going to come out on the other end of life unscathed. I never prepared myself for the worst, or even the not-so-nice parts of what were to come. I was in a blissful state of self-induced ignorance. I didn't want to entertain the idea that my dad would ever be in pain. But after surgery and while he was recovering, I cried quite a bit. I would chat with him for a couple hours and then go upstairs to my room, holding back tears until I could shut my door to ensure solace and privacy. I felt terrible that I couldn't take some of the pain from him to hold and hide—he had to deal with it all himself, and I despised how helpless I felt. For all the security my dad had always given me, I couldn't make him better in return.

Despite his decidedly negative decline in those short weeks of recovery, my dad came out on the other side relatively unscathed. The only marks his cancer left behind were a few fading incision scars and a little extra belly fat. Once he could get out of bed, he was up and raring to take on the world again sans prostate. He started doing yard work and lifting timber while on job sites, and he kept looking better and better. He started running again. He could break a sweat without worrying about messing up his stitches. Our dinner-table discussions stopped revolving around how he was feeling that day and became more about when we were all going to go pick peaches together.

My dad is an unwittingly amazing teacher. He taught me how to be strong even when I feel my weakest. He made me appreciate seventies disco music. He forced me to follow my instincts and wants in life until I get what I need. He instilled in me the fact that there's nothing better that a parent can do than listen to their mini-me's and read to them when they ask. Even if you've read Harry Potter to them more than twice. Finally, he taught me the value of being realistic. If my life was an ever-upward-pointing seesaw, his experiences dealing with cancer sat on the other side and leveled my optimism out. And I'm unexpectedly grateful for that. I don't take things for granted as often now, and I'm less likely to have unrealistic views of the future. He made me want to go to the doctor more often, which is saying something, since I'm a needle-hating, panicking animal every time I sit on an examination table. Thanks, Daddy-o. For listening first, and always letting me do my thing with only a light sigh when I'm heading toward a seemingly bad idea. I love you, and I'll eternally appreciate your altruistic parenting.

Seeing vulnerability and humanity in the person you idolize can be jarring and sad, but it is a necessary step to growing up. Knowing that my dad was a human being and not omnipotent was upsetting, but it also made me realize that I'm going to be just like him when I grow up. He's not superhuman; he doesn't have a secret to adulthood that I'll figure out one day. He's my dad. And I love him. And the love I feel for him makes me respect him, and one day, I'm going to evoke the same feeling in someone else. A feeling of trust and security. And if I want to be qualified enough to give other people life advice and be some sort of mentor, I better get my shit together. I have to start taking responsibility for my life, and so do you.

Adulting isn't a course you can take in college. Becoming an adult is a labor of time and failure. You've got to make some stupid decisions and spend too long doing activities you don't want to do in order to figure out the right choices and what you enjoy doing. I'm sure that's nearly the exact struggle my dad and every other prospective adult went through to become independent and noteworthy individuals. If adulthood could be sectioned out as a pie chart, 65 percent of the chart would be "doing things you hate doing," 20 percent would be "fun things that distract you from your generally nihilistic view of the world," 10 percent would be "talking to people and trying to maintain eye contact without looking like a serial killer," and 5 percent would be "trying to figure out if your hot water was shut off, or if the tap was just taking a while to heat up."

Growing up is a confusing vortex of wants and desires and the reluctance to take the actions to reach your wants and desires. Sure I want a tasteful six-pack. But that requires actually taking the time to move my inactive body until it screams in pain and sweats everywhere. It also requires that I give up essential parts of my diet. Like truffle-oil fries. And Marshmallow Fluff. It's all a balancing act of expectations, and social media has not helped with tipping the scales. Every time I go on Instagram I see some wasp-waisted mink of a lady doing squats to the camera. How am I supposed to feel like a real person when I'm exposed to that kind of beauty all the time?

That person must be working her ass off (or on) to get that body. What am I doing over here? And then I remember that little thing called "genetics" and I feel better.

After my dad recovered from surgery, he went into a mode of exploration and adventure that his young self would envy. He wanted to spend more time with his kids, he wanted to run around with us and take us to the local orchard. He just wanted to live life and enjoy everything he had worked so hard to achieve. His life has been a testament to the self-control and hard work he has exerted to be able to enjoy the fruits of his labor. He definitely had to go through some messy and unpleasant horrors in life, but he came out on the other side energized and ready to live with purpose. Your heroes are human (unless they are literally comic-book characters). You might actually be looked up to one day. Treat yourself like you can make a difference in someone else's life. I'm sure a young Jett Ricks never thought that his future daughter would be writing a chapter in a how-to book about his bravery and humanity in order to teach a bunch of young people about heroism.

A Short List of Places I've Cried in Public*

- In the parking lot of a Goodwill
- Putting change into a parking meter
- In the Chick-fil-A drive-through
- At a pet adoption fair (upward of three separate crying sessions during the event)
- Walking down the sidewalk, thinking about a paraplegic cat I saw on Instagram
- Filling up my gas tank
- Pulling up to the airport
- Leaving the airport
- Watching *Finding Dory* in theaters

*this list doesn't account for the thirty times I've cried while driving.

IT'S OKAY TO FEEL SAD. OR HAPPY. OR BOTH AT THE SAME EXACT TIME.

Emotions are weird, aren't they? As someone with a love/hate relationship with her hormones (mostly a hate relationship), I tend to feel extreme levels of feelings both positive and unpleasant. What I've learned through all the crying jags and overly emotional text messages sent at three a.m. is that feelings are just things. You can't help them; they aren't your fault; they just are. And that's mostly because feelings are totally uncontrollable. Want a quick example? Don't feel sadness and pity when you think about how many puppies will never have happy homes and families to enjoy. Okay, that was a bit dark. Let me try again. Don't feel adorable joy when you think about those same puppies playing with babies from their happy forever homes and licking the babies' chubby faces and making them laugh short little chortles. Now, STOP THINKING ABOUT HOW CUTE THEY ARE AND HOW THERE'S HOPE IN THE UNIVERSE. STOP THINKING ABOUT THE MANIFEST HAPPINESS OF ALL THOSE BABIES AND PUPPIES. STOP THAT RIGHT NOW. See? Harder than you think to control your emotions.

What I want you to know is that all these feelings we're feeling aren't good or bad—it's only our actions that can be positive or negative. In the wake of any emotion, you have the choice between good behavior and bad behavior. Let's say your dad eats the last ice-cream sandwich in the freezer and now you're upset. You have one of two options: Hex him with an ancient pirate curse that will leave him unfortunate for the rest of his life, or let that sandwich go in exchange for a scoop of your mother's sugar-free diet vanilla ice cream. Sure, the saccharine taste of aspartame and sadness will coat your tongue the moment that fake Tahitian *vanille* hits your palate, but at least you're being nice to your dear old dad. When you're mad, you could choose to take it out on others or your environment, but nine times out of ten, that's not the correct avenue. I'm not telling you to control your emotions—no one should have to wrangle or change how they feel—I'm just suggesting you control your reaction to emotions. You're better off letting your feelings do their thing.

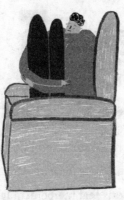

Even better, get a therapist. I can't tell you how life-changing it is to have a person in your life whose sole job is to listen to all your shit and make you feel slightly better by the end of a session, mostly by just repeating your questions back at you. Seriously. It's an odd feeling at first, but once you get used to the idea of a complete stranger knowing all your deepest, darkest secrets, you're totally capable of getting everything out there. You can take inventory of your mental well-being and understand the healthy and toxic sides of your psyche. For instance, I never knew that I struggled with obsessiveness until I saw a therapist. I was living in a state of willful ignorance, thinking my daily internal turmoil was Just a Girly Thing and not something I could be medicated for.

In fact, you might be surprised by how many people are on antidepressants. The *Journal of the American Medical Association* reports that the percentage of Americans on some form of antidepressant went from 6.8 percent in 1999 to 13 percent in 2012. So if you took a random sampling of one hundred Americans, thirteen of them would be taking mood-altering medication. And the actual number of people who would have been medicated with antidepressants in 2012 was 4,066,155 in the

United States alone. That's a pretty big chunk of people. I don't think this increase in medicating is necessarily a negative thing. With the rise of the internet and the inevitable increase in communication and understanding of others, people were bound to be more comfortable opening up about their issues. I mean, we no longer live in an era where housewives are brought to climax by doctors as a means of combatting hysteria. Though now that I'm a little older and have a long-distance boyfriend, I do see how that *technique* could help with stress.

The problem of not being believed, or of being told "you'll shake it off in a month," by a doctor is still a prevalent issue for people battling mental illnesses. I think that's one of the major dick moves a practicing doctor can pull. When someone comes into the office with a broken arm, they get taken seriously. If someone comes in feeling low or sad or not quite themselves, it's just a phase to move past. It's incredibly difficult to put into words what your brain and body are constantly at war about! When I'm really low, I feel like a bland bowl of oatmeal. No dried cranberries. No almond slivers. Forget the sexy drizzle of honey. I'm snotty, old, gray oatmeal. But my gray oatmeal feeling is such a complicated thing to communicate to someone I'm close to or respect. I have an easier time relaying my feelings to strangers on the internet (or those of you precious people reading this) than telling my doctor that my brain feels like a numb big toe. Which is a backward philosophy. I feel like I can't talk about struggling mentally because I don't know how to put it into words or because I'll worry people, and that is NOT a good way to think about your mental health. So many folks out there are sad! And so many psychologist folks out there want to hear about your sadness and help you with it!

I've learned that I need to treat my brain, feelings, and moods like limbs. If I was that girl with the broken arm, I'd be at my doctor's office in a jiff to get it looked at, cared for, put in a cast. As my good friend Drake once said, "a sprained ankle ain't nothin' to play with." But why can't I make the connection that depression can be just as detrimental as a wounded arm, if not more so? We humans have to better recognize the struggles we put ourselves through. Relying on a medication to stabilize our moods or the chemistry in our brains is a completely normal and acceptable way to live life. And it's good. As long as you're not abusing your prescriptions, medicine is there for a reason: to help us get through this cluster-fuck of anxiety and sadness we call life.

Wooo, that got heavy real fast. All I'm saying is: Give your brain a break. Use this moment in your day to check in on your head. Hey, beautiful. How's that glorious mind of yours doing? Does it need a nap? Need to take a chill pill? Go for it. Treat your mind and body as equals. You wouldn't let a broken arm heal on its own, so make sure to be giving your emotions, thoughts, and feelings proper time to heal when they need to—whether that means enrolling in therapy, going for morning walks by yourself to clear your head, or just listening to your favorite album when you're having a rough day. Give your brain a treat every now and then. It deserves it.

Here's another thing worth saying on the topic of emotions and mental-health well-being: you're allowed to be happy. I've had to combat a serious case of guilt nearly every time my life seems to be going in the right direction. I used to feel undeserving of positive events or people in my life, and I needed to get over those self-sabotaging vibes quickly if I was going to enjoy even a fraction of my success. You work and work and work for a better life, and then you're not allowed to appreciate it. That's been my brain's life philosophy since I was seventeen years old. I felt like I cheated the system by engaging in a job I loved doing, or finding a partner who fulfilled my every want and ask in a romantic relationship. Some weird, grotesque part of me would wait for disaster to strike. And I would dread the day everything would crumble around me. And then that day didn't come. I'm still here. Alive. And decently satisfied with what's going on in my world. I love my boyfriend. I love where I live. And I love the creative freedom that my work provides. I'm allowed to feel good about the places I'm going. So are you.

Don't listen to the little voice in your head saying that you're not worthy of happiness. Or that you're crazy. Or that you can't express your emotions. Everyone deserves to feel justified and content in their life. You're allowed to be proud of what you've done and what you're doing. You're allowed to feel sadness and despair. You're

allowed to be human. You need to start accepting com-
pliments and giving yourself a mental pat on the back
when you've accomplished something for yourself.
You need to rest and recover when you've had a rough,
emotionally taxing time.

You need to meditate. I know I sound like a crazy hip-
pie, but it's the only thing keeping me sane as I write this.
A short fifteen or twenty minutes of just sitting and letting
my brain decompress has become my everything. When
your to-do lists pile up and start feeling like should-have-
done lists, stop your life and take a breather for a second.
I never thought I would be some Californian stereotype,
what with my shaggy bangs and lack of breast support.
But here I am, nipples out, currently burning bras, and
calm of mind. Or at least getting calmer. I'm not saying
you need to run out and find religion, twelve different
sizes of rose quartz crystal, and discover the meaning of
life to become a relaxed individual. If you can sit in your

chair, put in some earbuds, close your eyes, and rest your mind for ten minutes, you're going to be shocked at how soothing it can be over time. This might be a phase I'm going through until my schedule doesn't induce panic deep within me every time I take notice of my calendar. Hopefully, it's a technique you and I can use to keep it cool and positive when life wants to suffocate us.

Also? Stop worrying all the time. I feel like I get stressed out over how everyone in my life is stressed out. Let's all just shut it down, people. Stress and worry are states of mind. You have control over whether you go on an intense crying jag of self-pity for five hours or whether you just get on with the damn thing. This doesn't mean you should dismiss your emotions (see above). Give them a nod and a moment to take over. Assess your emotions, decide which ones will get you through this particularly trying time, and don't let the negative ones cause you to spiral. You are the captain of your own ship, and it's your job to steer it in the right direction. I know you're not an old-school eye-patch-and-peg-leg pirate. But it's true.

This might make you feel like a slight crazy person at first, but repeating positive mantras to yourself when you're in a pinch can be lifesaving. If you say something enough, you start to believe it. When I'm nervous to do an audition, or I feel anxious about meeting some-one for the first time, I always repeat some damn nice things to myself. I'll talk about how I'm going to smash the read when I get in the audition room. How girls with glasses always get the quirky-cool roles. I'll remind myself that people are self-conscious. That person I'm about to introduce myself to? She's probably just as concerned about making a good impression. Be a positive realist. "But that's just an optimist, Arden." I KNOW. Let me explain.

Optimism is always seeing the bright side of things—noticing only the good and rejecting the decent chance that negative things are going to occur. Being a positive-minded realist means tackling the outcomes of an event you're nervous or worried about and boiling it down to logic. Half the time, you'll realize that you've been covertly negative and shooting yourself in the foot by only considering possible bad outcomes. Just think of the absolute worst thing and best thing that could happen when you're about to go on a date with your new coworker who's supercute and also smells faintly of pine and pencil erasers. He could take you to a sketchy dive bar and have nothing to talk about other than his five pet rats. He could also be the love of your life and sweep you off your feet, dancing you into the sunset after a romantic candlelit linguini sesh. Most likely, a middle ground between the two of these extremes will occur. Count on the realistic. Hope for the optimistic.

One of the most important things I want to stress to you, my precious shining star, is that your emotions are your own property. You can't hold other people responsible for them, but you also deserve to do what you need to in order to take care of them. If a friend always makes you feel bad, you can separate from that person. It's that easy. Whether that human being makes you feel anxious or not good enough or sad or unendingly envious, if you get the constant urge to cut all ties and forget they exist, stop spending your time with them. I wish I could reach back into my high school days and slap fifteen-year-old Arden in the face. Along with fourteen-, sixteen-, and seventeen-year-old Arden as well. I kept so many terribly toxic friendships because I was fearful of loneliness. I was constantly walking on eggshells, worried I wasn't going to be invited to the next sleepover. I felt paranoid that my "friends" were saying mean comments behind my back. I knew they were shit-talkers when they would gossip about each other with me. I would just spend the whole gross conversation wondering what atrocities they would spew about me later that night. I didn't want to leave them alone in a room for fear of them embarrassing me by ragging on my entire being.

Eventually, those friendships ended in a messy and degrading divorce. I was left feeling isolated and unwanted. I thought everyone had a terrible image of me, and I projected that same image onto myself. I wanted to blame every single girl who said I was a slut for breaking up with my boyfriend (yeah, that was an actual reason people came up with for being mean to me). I would have revenge dreams about exposing all of them for their snaky insides. I also dreamed about going full-blown *Parent Trap* and setting a million booby traps in their houses so they would wake up covered in fake spiders and maple syrup. But I never enacted my vengeance. I stewed and boiled away, poisoning myself with the grudge I had built up against those catty bitches. I would see pictures of them on Facebook from when they would all hang out, and then I would eat sweet and salty popcorn and cry.

Eventually, the only thing I could control in my life—not other people, not my family, not the weather, not whether boys liked me—was order. So I began treating my life rather obsessively. I would only eat three things a day. And by things I mean, like, three ingredients. Apple, bag of popcorn, slice of cheese might be one of the appetizing menus I would stick to. The one allowance on top of the three things was coffee, and I would drink it obsessively because I was so concerned about being thin; I wanted my metabolism to be revved up constantly. If I forgot to make coffee at home, I would beg the administrators to let me have coffee from the teachers' lounge. I was convinced my life would crumble around me if I didn't have coffee and three other food items during the day. No more, no less. It was a weird time for me.

I've heard from several other women who went through the same food control issues that this is a common coping mechanism. I restricted my eating to the point of being considered anorexic, but I never got scary thin. That's one common misconception about eating disorders. You don't have to be starving to death to have disordered eating. It's just a matter of making your food and eating habits a guilty, negative, or control-related activity that can constitute an eating problem. I regained a normal eating schedule after my mom pulled me aside and explained that I had to eat regularly like a normal human. She didn't threaten to ground me or punish me. The sheer fact that someone had noticed my eating made me self-conscious enough to eat around my family. Eventually I realized that controlling my food wasn't going to solve all my issues, and I regained a healthy lifestyle. But in the beginning it was rough. My trichotillomania only got worse; I would show up to school with marker eyebrows since I had no hairs left.

My parents got worried about me the summer after freshman year. I would sit inside my room all day, lying in bed and just hanging out on my laptop. YouTube was a kind of escape for me early on in my channel history. I would spend all day watching other people, filming videos, editing, or uploading. It was an amazing distraction. I felt productive, and because I was watching so many fascinating people online, I didn't feel lonely. I didn't think much then of my self-induced isolation, but in hindsight, I was avoiding confronting the outside world. I didn't want to talk to or see anyone from my school. I really hated the idea of running into my ex-friends in the real world. I remember going to the movies with my parents and realizing we were waiting to see the same movie as my old friends. I was mortified that these girls were going to see me out and about with Robin and Jett. And I felt even guiltier about being embarrassed of my parents. So I just subconsciously decided to never leave the house unless I was going for a drive around the block.

Between my mild agoraphobia, my OCD, and my lack of calorie intake, I was a real big ole mess. I can understand my parents justifying an intervention. When they confronted me about how I was acting and how I looked, I acted and looked shocked that they even considered I had a problem. How dare they judge me just like everyone else did! I was just fine! I was totally cool! I just needed to make sure that trail mix only had three ingredients in it and I'd be eating it quietly in my room for the next twelve hours, seething over their confrontation. I had allowed my issues to control me. I couldn't enjoy life because I was too busy blaming others and feeling scared of everyone. If I had just stepped back for a second and looked at the reality of my situation in proper lighting, I would have come to the swift realization that everyone at my age goes through this awkward period of awkwardness. Granted, I was struggling with OCD and disordered eating, but the actual issues causing my problems were very common teen issues. I was just wired to deal with them in a more extreme way. Everyone feels alienated at some point. Everyone feels strung out by the social order at their school. Not everyone pulls out their hair to deal with these things, but high school can be hard for anyone. You don't 100 percent know who you are, and you're constantly questioning everything. Everyone in your class is having a mild existential crisis at the same time, so it results in a messy sludge of teenagehood that will leave you begging to be thirty. Yes, if Snapchat is to be believed, it would seem like everyone is having the fucking TIME OF THEIR LIVES. Believe me when I say that they are not. But this period in your life doesn't last. You learn from your misery, grow thicker skin, and get a move on. You stop taking as much shit. You respect yourself and others more because you know what it feels like to be an outcast.

I wish I hadn't been so hard on myself. I wish I hadn't let other people get to me. But I'm glad that I struggled a little bit. Now I know my self-worth, and I know how little I should give a shit. Fuck letting other humans dictate your personal standards in life. Live and let live. I've learned to do my own thing, dance to my own drum, and seemingly not be bothered about what other people think. Obviously you can't entirely tune out the opinions and thoughts and feelings of others. You would be a sociopath if you did. But self-preservation is surprisingly unselfish. You can only be the best you if you take care of your physical and mental well-being. By being the ultimate form of yourself (the best version of myself is probably the equivalent of a fat and lazy house cat napping in the sun), you're helping others. You'll be at the top of your game and able to efficiently deal with the outside world with an unclouded mind.

Take it easy, kiddo. Go to the doctor when you need to. Visit your therapist regularly, or sign up for therapy pronto if you have a more stressful lease on life. Meditate when you feel overwhelmed. Meditate when you feel at ease. Realize that your constant anxieties and worries and personal pitfalls are all in your mind and that you are in control, even if you feel a bit nutty sometimes. Address your feelings like relatives; you're going to have to see them all every now and again, probably and especially at family reunions. Some of them you're very familiar with and get on with just fine. Others cause a complete scene and usually ruin all the festivities and make terrible pumpkin pie. You don't have to see that overly dramatic aunt who constantly rags on your very state of being all the time, but it's okay to entertain her for a short time. That emotion will pass on eventually. They all do. You'll never hit a point in your life, whether you're almost adulting or full-on adulting or nearing actual death, where an emotion isn't merely a temporary state of being. It's survivable. I promise.

We're tough as shit and we're going to make it.

MY WAY, OR A
VERY UNPLEASANT HIGHWAY

If you can't already tell, I spend a large portion of my life traveling. Planes, trains, cars, buses—you name it, I've slept awkwardly against a window in it. With several years of packing, unpacking, repacking, and re-unpacking under my belt, I've learned a thing or two about what is necessary to prepare for and bring on a trip. So, let's go through some of my top travel tips! I've managed to grow out of having a sweaty, shaking panic attack before every plane ride over thirty minutes long, which means I am undeniably qualified to give you advice.

First up, make some lists. Make several lists. Make as

many lists as you possibly can. In your mind, run through every product (hair, makeup, skin care, etc.) that you used in the last twenty-four hours. Those are the products you actually need to pack. Not that random mask you think you *might* use if you have a free hour before tapas with your friends. Not the three skin serums you got samples of two years ago that have probably expired. Learn to take only what you need. Also, take only the *quantity* that you need. Don't take a full shampoo bottle if you're only gone for a few days. Get yourself a couple mini travel bottles from your nearest drugstore and fill those little guys with everything: facial toner, shampoo, body wash, all your favorite items that you can't live without and that don't come in a travel size.

Figure out the climate of the place you're traveling to and make a list of the clothes you will absolutely wear. I don't mean pack for the end of the world. Pack for the easiest travel of your life. If you end up needing something like a dress or a shirt, we live in a world where H&M is an international brand. You *will* be able to find a store that sells decent clothes regardless of where you're going. Don't bring a bikini if you're going to Switzerland. Unless you're some kind of exposed-breast snowboarding masochist. Don't bring something "just in case" you need it, because I promise you that the "in case" never ever happens. I've packed so many bathing suits that have been crumpled up and crushed for months in forgotten suitcases. I've also shown up to the English countryside in the dead of winter and actually needed a bathing suit for some hot-tub-related activity. But guess what? I found a bathing suit within ten minutes of needing one at a store in the center of town for, like, twenty bucks. So why lug around extra baggage you may or may not need? Personally, I like to save ample room in my luggage for shopping, because I'm a realist. I know I'm going to want to buy ALL THE THINGS. So why would I pack all my old things? I shall buy new things instead. Obviously. This is travel logic.

But seriously. There's something to be said about leaving room for adventure. Even in your suitcase. You might end up wanting to take home a bulk sachet of lavender buds from France. Or a bunch of nesting dolls from eastern Europe (although I feel like those would pack up nicely). It might just be my personality, but I think it's more fun to leave yourself some space for unforeseen purchases. I've been on the receiving end of an overpacking bonanza that ended with all my fun, new foreign goods being thrown in the trash at border control because there was too much stuff. It's not an enjoyable experience. So take a good look at your suitcase after you've packed it: pull everything out and repack with a critical second round of scrutiny. Do I need two bottles of perfume? Or am I going to forget to put any of it on when I get to Auckland and start jumping into glowworm caves?

One of the most important rules I've learned in packing has been ROLL UP YOUR SHIT. Seriously. I adopted this popular form of organization a couple years ago and it's changed the game for me. No more wrinkly shirts and crammed-in underwear. Everything gets to have a tight little swirl that fits neatly next to a similar item. You can find tutorials on YouTube discussing the best techniques for this particular method, but I usually just take everything bottom to top and roll it up like a yoga mat. I've gotten so good at it that I can successfully roll a faux fur coat down to the size of a T-shirt.

Plane travel can be exhausting, draining, and traumatic (and if you're riding with United, we've learned it might even be violent), but it doesn't have to be! Well, yeah, it kind of does because you *are* in a giant metal airbus flying through the air with hundreds of other people jammed together sharing oxygen and food and space ohgodimgettingnauseous. BUT there are a few things you can do to make that eleven-hour flight feel like it's only slightly over six hours! First off, wear the comfiest thing you can think of. No one gives a shit what you look like. No one. Wear something that makes you feel like you're as close to hibernation as possible, and remember to layer. There's nothing worse than being in a stuffy airplane that's sitting on the tarmac, slowly heating to a million degrees, while wearing a sweatshirt you can't take off because you didn't even wear a bra underneath, let alone a T-shirt. So, layer. T-shirt, sweatshirt, jacket. Three layers. Always. If it's too hot, you can take it down a notch, but cold airplanes are the bane of my existence. You can always use your jacket as a little lap blanket if you're a weirdo like me and get cold legs constantly.

Next up, smear some oil on your face before your flight. Yup. Oil. On your face. It will make a barrier between your skin and the gross filtered air in the cabin. And it will keep you hydrated, so you don't get the life sucked out of your skin. It's an especially good idea if you have acne-prone skin, because it protects your face from outside forces coming and wrecking all that skin-care work you've been doing for the past month. I recommend using rosehip oil. You can even soak a couple cotton pads in the stuff and carry it on in a little plastic bag. Once it's on, don't touch your face. At all. Unless you want to risk contamination.

DON'T DRINK ANY LIQUIDS THAT AREN'T PREPACKAGED. If it doesn't come in a can or a bottle, don't drink it. I've been down a few rabbit holes online, and let me tell you, airlines do not give a shit about clean water. Don't trust the coffee, don't trust the tea . . . if you want to know why, read the Reddit forum about what airlines don't tell you. It's a doozy. Basically, the level of hygiene required to serve coffee or fresh beverages isn't so . . . fresh. You're better off bringing in iced coffee or tea packets.

This is beyond obvious, but bring your own snacks and drinks on your flight. You'll save money and your own health. You never know how long those prepackaged sandwiches have been hanging out in the service fridge. Once again, not worth the risk of getting food poisoning on a metal bird hurtling through the air.

Last, but certainly not least, bring your own entertainment. Obviously, airlines have the beauty of TV screens at most seats, with a surprisingly good selection of movies and TV to watch. However, if you're like me and you're traveling every couple months, you start catching up on the new flow of movies. You run out of suitable shows to watch and end up playing the weird short films that are for some reason included in the entertainment packages on every flight. Charge up your phone, download your favorite Netflix shows, and only use low battery mode so you can binge as many episodes as possible. Save yourself the trouble of worrying about what you're going to watch on the plane and download it beforehand, dummy!

Now, let's move on to some advice about my favorite part of traveling: your lodging. Have you already picked what country you want to go to? Dope. Do you have an idea of the city or countryside that interests you? Awesome. Have you thought about what kind of experience you want to have while you're there, though? Do you want an upscale hotel that can feed you grapes while someone massages your feet and tells you how special you are? Or do you want to be independent and able to run around from

Airbnb to Airbnb? The place and area that you're staying in are just as important as the activities you plan on doing when you get there. Personally, I'm usually a bit more freewheeling, which lends itself toward an Airbnb style of travel. Being able to roll up to a homey lodging after a long day of running around and sightseeing is really appealing to me, and it's cheaper!

I'd seriously consider looking at Airbnbs anywhere you're planning on going. They allow you to live like a local and see the city from the eyes of someone who experiences it on the daily. Will and I went with a bunch of our friends on a trip to Scotland for a couple days. We ended up using Airbnb and booked this insane farmhouse in the countryside for a crazy cheap price. We could have easily gotten a crappy hotel for the same rate and would have ended up having half the fun. We used every inch of the house to play sardines (a bunch of drunk twentysomethings effectively playing hide-and-seek in the middle of the Scottish countryside is a sight to see, let me tell you), and we had a blast.

By the same token, if you're already an avid Airbnb-er, read every review. This is true of any travel accommodations, but make sure that everyone who has previously stayed at your lodgings has had a good time. I've been an overly optimistic person too many times when it comes to travel, and your best bet is to rely on other people to tell you the truth about their experiences. Don't ignore complaints. You will regret it. And don't book a place that has no reviews if it seems too good to be true. It's typically a wise idea to go with a place that's seen a few people walk through its doors. You don't want to be the person who has to leave the review about the cockroach problem.

This is an incredibly millennial thing to say, but once you get there, take pictures!!! Take video!! Capture everything you can! But stop worrying about posting it on social media constantly. Enjoy the pictures and videos you take for yourself rather than worrying about how many people will like the Instagram of you pretending to take a bite out of a giant cheese wheel. Have a record of what happened, but don't worry about how many other people will see it. Our generation has become obsessed with letting others into every aspect of our lives, but sometimes it's nice to record or capture memories just for ourselves. It doesn't always have to be tainted with a filter and whacked up on Twitter to be scrutinized by our peers.

Traveling is a luxury few people can afford, and you

should remember that. It's awesome that you get to go on vacation, or get to experience a new culture or country. It's important to stay grounded and try to appreciate every bit of your adventure. Take it all in, and jam-pack your days with as many awesome activities as you can fit in. Trust me, you can always skip a yoga class in the mountains or that snow-water glacial facial, but you'll be glad you booked them in advance. Remember to pack your clothes light, and your days heavy.

Have fun, kiddos!

ACKNOWLEDGMENTS

This book was made possible mostly by people other than myself. Sure, I wrote the damn thing, but there was a dedicated group of people in the background making sure I was turning in pages rather than turning into a puddle of procrastination and self-pity. Thank you to my manager, Byron, for watching over this writing process. Thank you for pretending to believe me when I would lie and say I was up to my neck in finished pages when I had obviously been playing video games for the last week and had no work to show for it. Thank you for coordinating all of the calls, hundreds of emails, and end-less barrage of Google docs that this book demanded. You the bomb, bazzeroni.

Thank you to my dear editor, Sara, for trusting my writing abilities more than you probably should have. You were so kind throughout the process, and while you probably wanted to wring my neck on several occasions, thank you for leaving my body intact, even when I turned in pages late. You made writing a book a surprisingly stress-free experience, and I can't thank you enough for the gentle encouragement you provided throughout this whole process.

Thank you to my lawyer, Jess, for looking out for my best interests and working tirelessly to make sure this was a safe investment of everyone's time. I know you were always there in the background. Like a beautiful legal safety net. Thank you.

Giant, huge, enormous thanks to my boyfriend, Will. You put up with my stressed-out self and always made me feel better when I wanted to break down. Thank you for reading my book like three times since I made you check over all of my writing obsessively. You rubbed my back and let me sit in silence for hours when I was in the home stretch and deadlines were looming. Love you, little worm.

Gotta give a thanks to my family. My love for critical thinking and literature was developed entirely by my mom, dad, and siblings. Dad, thanks for letting me sit in your lap and "help" you with the Sunday crosswords. Those learning sessions have helped me pose as a smart person for most of my adult life. Mom, thanks for always being a goofball and teaching me what good storytelling sounds like. I regularly left the dinner table with tears and sides splitting when you felt like telling the hilarious misfortune that your day held for you.

And lastly, thank you to the subscribers, followers, and other amazing people who interact with me online. You guys have actively shaped my future since I was fourteen years old. My younger self could never have guessed the amount of love and support I would feel in the coming years from the multitudes of awesome people that watch my content. I couldn't ask for a more encouraging, intelligent, and engaging group of people to follow me. Thank you. Thank you for making this book, and my entire career, possible.